Howard Richards.

Dec, 1986.

The Wisden Book of Cricket Quotations

THE
WISDEN
BOOK OF
CRICKET
QUOTATIONS

Edited by
David Lemmon

Queen Anne Press
Macdonald & Co
London & Sydney

Illustrations reproduced by kind permission of

BBC Hulton Picture Library (pages 22, 46, 78, 185)
The Mansell Collection (pages 38, 44, 49, 56, 82, 86, 149, 169)
Marylebone Cricket Club (pages 11, 15, 27, 52, 95, 122, 131)

Photograph of David Lemmon by *John Alexander Studio*

First published in 1982 by Queen Anne Press, Macdonald & Co (Publishers) Ltd, Maxwell House, 74 Worship Street, London EC2A 2EN.

Printed and bound in Great Britain by Hazell Watson & Viney Ltd, Aylesbury, Bucks

Contents

Introduction

In his introduction to *The Oxford Dictionary of Quotations*, Bernard Darwin, not unknown to lovers of cricket, anticipated a complaint.

'It is safe to say' he wrote, 'that there is no single reader who will not have a mild grievance or two, both as to what has been put in and what has been left out. In particular he will "murmur a little sadly" over some favourite that is not there. I, for instance, have a small grievance. William Hepworth Thompson, sometime Master of Trinity, the author of many famous and mordant sayings on which I have been brought up, is represented by but a single one.'

Bernard Darwin leads us straight to the weakness, and strength, of any compilation of this nature – the personal taste which must pervade the selection, pleasing some and dismaying others. It would be as well, then, to begin with an explanation of the criteria on which this selection was made.

In the first place, the quotations included in this volume have their origin in literature – the literature of the game itself most obviously, but also the novel, the play, the essay, the poem and the autobiography in which the game of cricket is mentioned only in passing or may even be used simply in the evocation of an image. The consistent factor is that each of the quotations in this collection may be verified by reference to the original, the written word. This stipulation allows no place for the apocryphal story which, although it may be often quoted at cricket dinners, has a lack of authenticity and an indeterminate source.

In one of my first books about cricket, for example, I told of Eddie Paynter going out to bat at The Oval in 1938 with over 500 runs on the board and ascribed to him the saying, 'Cometh the hour, cometh the man. Just the man for a crisis.' One reviewer, a distinguished and cultured man, took me to task on this, asserting that the words were spoken by Cliff Gladwin in South Africa in December 1948 when he and Alec Bedser scrambled a win off the last ball of the first Test. Had I had the opportunity to reply, I might have said, as Sir Neville Cardus surely would have, 'If Paynter didn't say those words, he should have done.'

Sayings and stories like these, and the many attributed to the young Fred Trueman, have become part of the folklore of the game, but like the doings of King Arthur, Robin Hood and El Cid they are of the stuff of dreams. This purports to be a book of facts although, hopefully, it is not without a hint of romance and humour.

The wealth of literature which confronts a compiler when he begins a work of this nature is quite daunting and I decided not to include quotations from newspapers and magazines unless they had been republished in book form as had *The Times* celebration of the M.C.C. in 1937 and much of Cardus. There are special exceptions to this rule, notably the origin of the 'Ashes' reference. With the source of each quotation, I have attempted to give the date of first publication or the date of publication of the text from which I worked, which is the case with *The Badminton Library – Cricket* (1904).

Sentences earn their inclusion for their pithiness, succinctness, literary elegance or simply because they are recognised as *bon mots*.
As we anticipated through Bernard Darwin, not everyone will be without a grievance and many will question why there are so many references to Grace, Emmett and Maclaren and so few to Botham, Boycott and Gooch. The answer lies in the words that these great players have inspired in others – it is no reflection of the esteem, or lack of it, in which they are held by the cricket lovers of today.

If I may take this point a little further, I would suggest that ultimately we quote to voice 'What oft was thought, but n'er so well expressed.' We become capable of articulating our loves through the words of Shakespeare or Andrew Marvell and talk about winning friends and influencing people without recording our debt to Dale Carnegie for the phrase. It would not be too outrageous to conjecture that in the next few years someone will suggest that had Botham been born in Ancient Greece, the *Iliad* would have been a different book, or that had he lived in the Middle Ages, he would have been a Crusader. The words, of course, were originally intended as a tribute to W. G. Grace, but every age has its giants and there are fewer changes than we think. Slowing the game down when things were not going well was advocated 150 years ago.

Each quotation is accredited to the author of the book from which it was taken, although one is aware that in some cases, such as Lord Hawke's *Recollections and Reminiscences*, the 'author' has received a certain amount of help. In general, the 'ghosted' autobiography has been avoided.

The selection completed, the problem that confronts the compiler is one of classification. I have rejected the standard method of arrangement by author and have used instead a form of thematic tabulation. Within each category I have attempted to place together sentences which complement or contradict each other so that the reader may savour something of the perpetual debate and exchange of opinion which is a vital ingredient of the game.

It is inevitable that one develops favourites. There is a pungency in the prose of Ranjitsinhji's *The Jubilee Book of Cricket* that has a captivating naivety (Did he really believe that a slovenly fielder should be thrashed?) and there is an elegance in Swanton, Altham and Carew that makes a large representation of their work essential to the fabric of this book. There is the wisdom and strength of Arlott and the vibrant humanity of Robertson-Glasgow, Peebles and Prittie which demand their inclusion, but I hope that readers will discover some lesser-known names in whose words they can delight.

There are some writers, of course, who are fully represented on the strength of one book. *Beyond a Boundary* by C. L. R. James is widely recognised as one of the very great cricket books and has been reissued several times since it was first published nearly 20 years ago, but a book with which younger readers may not be familiar is *The Complete Cricketer* by A. E. Knight which was published in 1906. Albert Ernest Knight was a Leicestershire professional who played three times for England. He was a widely read man and a Methodist lay preacher who would pray before he went in to bat and often, it was said, while batting. His book is written with an Edwardian grandeur and ecclesiastical dignity that made it difficult not to include every sentence in this collection. The temptation was finally resisted, but this confession may help to explain why Knight is so well represented here.

The decision to adopt a form of thematic classification of the quotations left the problem of a guide to easy reference so, to aid the reader, there are two points of reference in the index; key word and author.

There is one book which is not represented in this collection and yet without it, this book would not have been possible. I refer, of course, to *The Bibliography of Cricket* compiled by E. W. Padwick for The Library Association and The Cricket Society. No serious work on cricket could be completed without reference to this monumental accomplishment.

Perhaps I may be allowed to draw one final analogy. On reflection, I saw myself as something resembling a Test selector. What he chooses does not please everyone. Some are insulted by his inclusions, others are offended by his omissions. All he can do is to stand firm and hope that he has chosen a winning side.

David Lemmon
Leigh-on-Sea
1983

Preparation and Practice

Out of the thousands of batsmen who have played cricket, it would be difficult to find two who stand exactly alike.

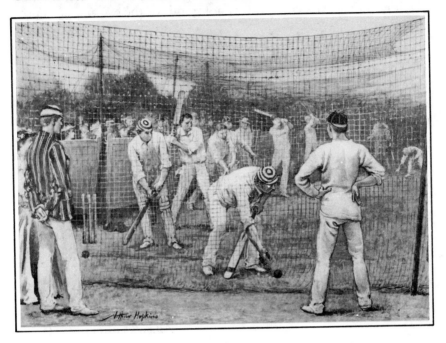

1. Years lost in early life are irrecoverable, particularly where cricket is concerned.

Leslie Ames
Close of Play (1953)

2. Temperance in food and drink, regular sleep and exercise, I have laid down as the golden rule from my earliest cricketing days.

W. G. Grace
The Badminton Library – Cricket (1904)

3. Let me say, however, that I never smoked until my day's cricket was done, and never drank anything except water for lunch when playing in a match. I do not think I am a bit old-fashioned in my opinion that there is too much smoking amongst those actually playing in first-class cricket. It is not good for the eye and does not strengthen the nerves – and nerves play more havoc than even the most devastating fast bowler on the other side.

    Lord Hawke
    Recollections and Reminiscences (1924)

4. No professional drunkard has ever made a great professional cricketer, nor ever will.

    'Quid'
    Jerks in from Short Leg (1866)

5. All cricketers in their teens, aye, and afterwards, who wish to improve their batting will do themselves a great deal of good by swinging Indian clubs.

    E. H. D. Sewell
    Well Hit! Sir (1947)

6. Don't practise on opponent's ground before match begins. This can only give them confidence.

    Sir J. M. Barrie
    Allahakbarries C.C. (1899)

7. In the first place, success in cricket, and not in cricket alone, depends on the enjoyment and interest taken in the game, and we believe that there is a great danger of destroying this enjoyment and interest by incessant coaching and teaching at too early an age. In the second place, all coaching has a tendency at first to eradicate individual peculiarities and to cramp a natural style.

    R. A. H. Mitchell
    The Badminton Library – Cricket (1904)

8. Coaching which is good, simply sharpens up a player, as wide travel and experience will.

    A. E. Knight
    The Complete Cricketer (1906)

9. To my mind there are amenities in coaching, and if boys are either unduly scolded or drilled into unduly careful methods when batting, the only result is to sicken them of the game.

Lord Hawke
Recollections and Reminiscences (1924)

10. Coaching is often very necessary, but great care must be taken not to curb a young player's natural shots, which are often his chief scoring strokes.

Leslie Ames
Close of Play (1953)

11. Nor should a coach try to make a pupil too steady a bat if he shows an inclination to hit out. Let him make the best of his material, and try not to change the boy's natural style, attributes or gifts by forcing them into a fixed groove.

K. S. Ranjitsinhji
The Jubilee Book of Cricket (1897)

12. To stand ideally is either to inflict upon yourself a form of astigmatism or of painful neck wrenching.

A. E. Knight
The Complete Cricketer (1906)

13. To this we can only rejoin, that out of the thousands of batsmen who have played cricket, it would be difficult to find two who stand exactly alike.

Hon. R. H. Lyttleton
The Badminton Library – Cricket (1904)

14. The present standard of coaching must somehow be improved. I am sure that today some coaching does more harm than good. Too many coaches try and turn out every player to a certain pattern. They don't encourage individuality or bring out their strong points.

R. E. S. Wyatt
Three Straight Sticks (1951)

15. I should like to say that good batsmen are born, not made; but my long experience comes up before me, and tells me that it is not so.

W. G. Grace
Cricket (1891)

16. I found myself reflecting on the blessings and curses of the natural aptitudes, those which bestow an innate athleticism, a ball sense, that seemingly effortless power that denotes perfect timing, that physical co-ordination which is quite instinctive and, though cultivated, can never be taught.

Ted Dexter and Clifford Makins
Testkill (1976)

Batting

No one is so lonely as a batsman facing a bowler supported by ten fieldsmen and observed by two umpires.

17. In the game of cricket it has always been customary to accord more adulation to batsmen than to bowlers.

I. A. R. Peebles
Talking of Cricket (1953)

18. Bowlers and wicket-keepers, however brilliant, cannot by the nature of their work captivate the spectator in quite the same way as the greatest batsmen.

E. W. Swanton
A History of Cricket – Volume Two (1962)

19. Of the many facets presented by the game of cricket, most men will agree that batting is the one most distinctly enjoyable and instinctively delightful.

A. E. Knight
The Complete Cricketer (1906)

20. Oo am I to be put off my stroke, Mum, becos a
            few 'ooligans boos?
    An Englishman's crease is 'is castle; I shall stay
            'ere as long as I choose.

Hubert Phillips
An Englishman's Crease

21. So let me go what'er befall,
    And I will make a score;
    I should not love thee, dear, at all,
    Loved I not batting more.

Alfred Cochrane
To Lucasta in *Collected Verses* (1903)

22. . . . it is as well for us to remember when we are watching the best
    batsmen that, however easy it may all look, they do not achieve
    their success without toil and sweat, and that there are times even
    with the greatest when they must seem to themselves, as we humble
    performers so frequently seem to ourselves, to be batting with a
    broomstick, with a barn door for a wicket.

E. W. Swanton
Denis Compton: A Cricket Sketch (1948)

23. Cricket is a most precarious profession; it is called a team game but,
    in fact, no one is so lonely as a batsman facing a bowler supported
    by ten fieldsmen and observed by two umpires to ensure that his
    error does not go unpunished.

John Arlott
An Eye for Cricket (1979)

24. The bowler has ten aides in the field, but they are helpless to act
    until that swift cut and thrust, that intensely private moment
    between batsman and bowler, is done. This numerical advantage of
    players to the bowling side, however, creates a situation which is
    almost unique to cricket. It makes batting, consequently the scoring
    of runs, an act of defiance by one man against a vastly superior
    force who control the ball at all times, except in that split second
    when it touches the bat.

Geoffrey Moorhouse
The Best-Loved Game (1979)

25. A run is more difficult to make than to save, because batting is in its nature a far less certain and reliable thing than bowling and fielding.

K. S. Ranjitsinhji
The Jubilee Book of Cricket (1897)

26. Scoring greatly diminished when round-arm bowling was thoroughly established, and increased again as grounds got better.

Hon. R. H. Lyttleton
The Badminton Library – Cricket (1904)

27. To be a good judge of a ball's length is a source of strength in any player, and a strictly accurate player seldom makes the mistake of playing forward when he ought to play back, and *vice versa*.

Ib.

28. I do not believe so implicitly, as some cricketers and writers upon cricket do, in watching the bowler's hand. I prefer to watch the ball, and not anticipate events.

W. G. Grace
W.G. – Cricketing Reminiscences and Personal Recollections (1899)

29. It is impossible for forward play to be quite as safe as back play, because there must be a moment when the ball is out of sight.

K. S. Ranjitsinhji
The Jubilee Book of Cricket (1897)

30. Any fool can play forward, but it is only the good player who can score off forceful back strokes.

A. C. Maclaren
The Young Batsman in *The Cricketer* (1921)

31. The hardest tests in batting are to play fast bowling on a fiery wicket and spin bowling on a sticky one.

Sir Pelham Warner
Lord's 1787–1945 (1946)

32. A batsman who cannot make runs on turf after rain and sun and wind is only half a batsman.

E. H. D. Sewell
Well Hit! Sir (1947)

33. Bad balls, particularly when straight, ought not to be treated with contempt.

K. S. Ranjitsinhji
The Jubilee Book of Cricket (1897)

34. In conclusion, never treat a straight ball with contempt, however badly bowled.

W. G. Grace
The Badminton Library – Cricket (1904)

35. The main stock-in-trade of any side is its playing strength and reserves.

J. H. Morgan
Glamorgan (1952)

36. Every cricketer knows that in the early stages of a batsman's innings – i.e. before he gets his eye in – luck plays an important part.

W. G. Grace
W.G. – Cricketing Reminiscences and Personal Recollections (1899)

37. Luck plays a big part in cricket. The greatest of players will experience a lean period, then a missed chance will enable form to be recovered in a match. One decent innings is better than all the net practice in the world.

Sir Donald Bradman
Farewell to Cricket (1950)

38. Unlike tennis players who enjoy a knock-up on court, the Test batsman, even after net practice, is still forced to use the first few overs in the middle as a warm-up.

Ted Dexter and Clifford Makins
Testkill (1976)

39. It is one of the compensations of batting at the highest level that the totally random element of selection ball by ball is, to some extent, mitigated by a state of exceptional awareness.

Ib.

40. Every position has its special charm.
You go in first and find as a reward
The wicket at its best; you go in later
And find the fielders slack, the bowling loose.

A. A. Milne
An Average Man in *The Day's Play* (1910)

41. If you go in first, let two of your most safe and steady players be put in, that you may stand a chance of 'milling' the bowling in the early part of the game.

> John Nyren
> *The Young Cricketer's Tutor* (1833)

42. Men are not made of brown paper: I have seen many kinds of bowling I could not play, but never one I would not face; nor would I give a farthing for a cricketer who does not play with the opinion that a ball cannot hurt him.

> G. T. Knight (1828)
> Letter quoted in William Denison's *Sketches of the Players* (1846)

43. They had only one standard by which to measure the merit of an innings, and that was its actual duration in time.

> Rex Warner
> *Escapade* (1933)

44. But it may with truth be said that the keen pleasure which is realised by every cricketer worthy of the name, while he is actually at the wickets, prevents him from feeling fatigue as an inconvenience until the innings is over.

> Hon. R. H. Lyttleton
> *The Badminton Library – Cricket* (1904)

45. Miriam: I don't know if I prefer Rog to have a good innings or a bad one: If it's a good one, he re-lives it in bed, shot by shot, and if it's a bad one he actually replays the shots until he gets it right. He can make a really good innings last all winter.

> Richard Harris
> *Outside Edge* (Act Two) (1979)

46. I dream of many a glorious drive,
I feel the cut that goes for five:
I hear the crowd's applauding roar
That follows oft a hit for four.
I practise the entrancing glide,
And win the battle for my side;
We rarely fail to make a stand
When I go in – in Fairyland.

> E. B. V. Christian
> *Dreams that I Dream* in *At the Sign of the Wicket* (1894)

47. There is an order of batsmanship which we feel it impossible to teach, which moves us to despair as well as to wonder by its marvellous eccentricities.

A. E. Knight
The Complete Cricketer (1906)

48. Perhaps the happiest scoring mood is that of a man, keen and careful, tinged with anxiety to do well, but conscious of his power.

Ib.

49. You might say that balance and timing add up to rhythm, and that it is rhythm which the unsophisticated spectator is appreciating when an especially delicious stroke evokes murmurs of 'Lovely, sir, lovely!'

E. W. Swanton
Denis Compton: A Cricket Sketch (1948)

50. There is no less technical skill in the delicate leg-glance and the accurate on-side placement than in the off-drive and the late cut, but there is much smaller spectatorial reaction.

J. M. Kilburn
Thanks to Cricket (1972)

51. A true batsman should in most of his strokes tell the truth about himself.

Sir Neville Cardus
Cricket (1930)

52. The great batsman lifts us out of our utilitarian selves: we admire his work for its beauty, not merely for its value in runs.

Sir Neville Cardus
The Summer Game (1929)

53. Ideally, the best batsman is he who can get the most runs in the most beautiful way and in the quickest time.

A. E. Knight
The Complete Cricketer (1906)

54. Give me the batsman who squanders his force on me,
Crowding the strength of his soul in a stroke;

E. V. Lucas
The Cricket Ball Sings (1899)

55. Even the most misanthropic critic must succumb to the smacking concussion of the full-blooded hit, to the fascination of the red ball rocketing into the blue sky, with its whirring flight of a driven partridge and its final crash as it lands on roof or window.

Hon. T. C. F. Prittie
Mainly Middlesex (1947)

56. The big hit – for six – is the most companionable of cricketing acts.

John Arlott
An Eye for Cricket (1979)

57. If you have legs, in the name of goodness use them. Spring out of your confined territory, and drive forward with all your might, with all your strength and with all your skill.

Nicholas Wanostrocht
Felix on the Bat (1845)

58. The great thing in hitting is, not to be half-hearted about it; but when you make up your mind to hit, to do it as if the whole match depended upon that particular stroke.

W. G. Grace
Cricket (1891)

59. Now, our country lads, accustomed to the flail or the hammer (your blacksmiths are capital hitters), have the free use of their arms; they know how to move their shoulders; and they can move their feet too – they can run; then they are so much better made, so much more athletic, and yet so much lissomer – to use a Hampshire phrase, which deserves at least to be good English.

Mary Russell Mitford
Our Village (1824–32)

60. He has knocked down the wicket
And broke the stumps,
And runs without shoes to save his pumps.

William Blake
An Island in the Moon (1787)

61. Who is to say that there are not moments in a boy's life when quickness of hand and eye, backed by courage and a broad pair of shoulders, do not authorise a little risk?

Frederick Gale
About a Tune on an Old Fiddle

Our country lads are so much better made, so much more athletic, and yet so much lissomer.

62. Noah was a good batsman, and a most severe hitter; by the way, I have observed this to be a common quality in left-handed men.

John Nyren
The Young Cricketer's Tutor (1833)

63. It would not do for everybody to be a hard hitter, nor for every one to be a stonewaller, but it should be remembered that batsmen who get runs quickly and play freely all round the wicket are not only more appreciated by the onlookers, but are often, by their rapid scoring, able to snatch a victory for their side when time is short and runs are needed.

W. G. Grace
W.G. – Cricketing Reminiscences and Personal Recollections (1899)

64. He blocked the doubtful balls, missed the bad ones, took the good ones, and sent them flying to all parts of the field.

Charles Dickens
Pickwick Papers (1837)

65. If you are the last man at the wicket, and if the game should be running very close, there is the greater reason for you to exercise the greater caution – by caution I do not mean timidity.

Nicholas Wanostrocht
Felix on the Bat (1845)

66. Defend until the excitement of your important position in the game shall subside.

Ib.

67. Today, dull batting has become so universally applied an accusation that one is apt to forget that cricket is the professional's livelihood, and for him the price of failure may be penury.

Hon. T. C. F. Prittie
Mainly Middlesex (1947)

68. There has grown up in late years a most deplorable practice amongst batsmen of leaving balls on the off side alone, for fear of risking their wickets.

A. G. Steel
The Badminton Library – Cricket (1904)

69. Another consolation is to remember that each fresh batsman is a fresh beginning to the game. He comes in unready, a hope to the bowler.

E. F. Benson and Eustace H. Miles
The Cricket of Abel, Hirst and Shrewsbury (1903)

70. The origin of words is always interesting, and some readers may be surprised to know that William Barnes was the inventor of the term 'stonewaller'. It was in 1882 that R. G. Barlow, playing for Lancashire v. Nottingham, made his famous record of five runs in two hours and a half's play. After the innings Barnes went up to Barlow and said, 'Bowling at you is like bowling at a stone wall!' The name stuck to Barlow, who, though not the first to play slow cricket, was literally the first 'stonewaller' of the cricket-field.

W. G. Grace
W.G. – Cricketing Reminiscences and Personal Recollections (1899)

71. A field of outsiders are always going in to bowl at the Public Service, and we block the balls.

Charles Dickens
Little Dorrit (1857)

72.   And the clock's slow hands go on,
And you still keep up your sticks;
But oh for the lift of a smiting hand,
And the sound of a swipe for six!
Block, block, block,
At the foot of thy wickets, ah, do!
But one hour of Grace or Walter Read
Were worth a week of you!
George Francis Wilson (of W. Scotton v. Australia)
Cricket Poems (1905)

73.   Judgement as to how and when to run is one of the characteristics
of a good batsman.
W. G. Grace
Cricket (1891)

74.   Further, I would say that in the very highest class of cricket running
between wickets can be 20 per cent of the art of batsmanship.
E. W. Swanton
Denis Compton: A Cricket Sketch (1948)

75.   'Yes!' – A batsman's response to his colleague's call to run.
A. E. Knight
The Complete Cricketer (1906)

76.   Run, run, run, the ball's a-rolling,
Scarcely to the boundary she'll go;
And the throwing's getting wild, and the wicket-keeper's riled,
So we'll try and steal another for the throw.
Horace G. Hutchinson
Song

77.   We lose our wicket most frequently not by pace from pitch or great
break or even huge swerve, valuable as such possessions are to a
bowler: these qualities in bowling may complete our defeat or
render it more certain; but we have been beaten essentially by our
own defective judgment.
A. E. Knight
The Complete Cricketer (1906)

78. How many who play cricket in their dreams have suffered the actual nightmare of not being able to find bat and gloves when one's turn comes: or even descending pavilion stairs and being unable to find the door that leads out on to the field.

E. W. Swanton
Denis Compton: A Cricket Sketch (1948)

79. His bat hangs in the dark pavilion lone,
Unheeded through each dreary winter day,
But in the summer one may chance to stay
A moment when the eager throng has flown,
And seeing it, may think of him who's gone;
And half recalling the dim past, may say:
'Twas with that bat that here I saw him play –
How well! – a hundred times.'

E. B. V. Christian
Hic Iacet in *At the Sign of the Wicket* (1894)

80. Closer, the bowler's arm swept down,
The ball swung, pitched and darted,
Stump and bail flashed and flew;
The batsman pensively departed.

John Arlott
Cricket at Worcester, 1938

81. Out – beyond question or wrangle!
Homeward he lurched to his lunch!
His bat was tucked up at an angle,
His great shoulders curved to a hunch.

Sir Arthur Conan Doyle
A Reminiscence of Cricket (1922)

82. His record, take it all in all,
Was not a very great one;
He seldom hit a crooked ball
And never stopped a straight one.

Anonymous
The Rabbit

83. They do not bowl me off my pad,
     No catches from my glove are had:
     The hated 'leg before' is banned
     In matches played in Fairyland.

E. B. V. Christian
Dreams that I Dream in *At the Sign of the Wicket* (1894)

84. In cricket, as spectators know,
     There's one unwritten law,
     Whatever way a batsman's out,
     He's never leg before!

F. B. Wilson
Leg Before in *Sporting Pie* (1922)

85. Men fall victims often to the mere bumping and the accidents of the
     game.

James Pycroft
Oxford Memories – Volume Two (1886)

86. He once practised for some match till he appeared to all the bowlers
     about Lord's to have reduced batting to a certainty: but when the
     day came, amidst the most sanguine expectations of his friends, he
     made no runs.

James Pycroft
The Cricket Field (1851)

87. He was a fast bowler. I went in first, and scoring seventy runs with
     some severe blows on the legs – nankeen knees and silk stockings,
     and no pads in those days – I consulted a friend and knocked down
     my own wicket, lest the match should last till the morrow, and I be
     stiff and unable to play.

James Pycroft (quoting Budd)
The Cricket Field (1851)

Bowling

88. It has been said that bowlers, like poets, are born not made.

I. A. R. Peebles
Talking of Cricket (1953)

89. The teaching of bowling is an art so difficult that pages of weighty instruction and learned diagrams have gone almost for nothing.
R. C. Robertson-Glasgow
Cricket Prints (1943)

90. The art of bowling is an incommunicable natural gift which can be perfected to almost any degree by practice.
K. S. Ranjitsinhji (quoting Kempson)
The Jubilee Book of Cricket (1897)

91. Bowling, like everything worth doing, takes a lot of careful practice before it can be expected to meet with success.
A. G. Steel
The Badminton Library – Cricket (1904)

92. Of course the bowler is born – who isn't? But whether or no he may be made if the right means be adopted, remains to be ascertained by experiment, the only teacher.
E. F. Benson and Eustace H. Miles
The Cricket of Abel, Hirst and Shrewsbury (1903)

93. A bowler requires not only an uncommonly good eye in order to aim straight at his target and judge his distance, but an exceptionally strong sense of rhythm.
C. S. Marriott
The Complete Leg-Break Bowler (1968)

94. The majority of cricketers who play for pleasure prefer batting to bowling, and shirk the hard work which is the only road to accuracy and length.
E. R. Wilson
Bowling

95. Mr E. M. Dawson, up to the age of fourteen, used to bowl for half an hour a day in the holidays, even in the winter, and on one occasion had his bowl after 28 degrees of frost! At seventeen, when at Harrow, he was fit to bowl for the Gentlemen. Unfortunately he afterwards learned to bat.
Ib.

96. Bowling consists of two parts: there is the mechanical, and the intellectual part. First you want the hand to pitch where you please and then the head to know where to pitch, according to the player.

James Pycroft
The Cricket Field (1851)

97. The Bowler
The three best qualities in this important person in the game are, a high delivery, an upright body, and for his balls to be pitched a proper length.

John Nyren
The Young Cricketer's Tutor (1833)

98. If you have one slow, and one fast bowler, pitch your wickets right up and down the wind. A slow bowler can never bowl well with the wind in his face. If your bowling is all fast and your opponents have a slow bowler, pitch your wickets with a cross wind, that you may in some degree destroy the effect of the slow bowling.

Ib.

99. The bowler being human is but clay, to be moulded by the works of his hand and brain, by the time and experience which agglutinate them, but, having the innate gift, he is not bound up with the band of our rules and regulations. A man is either a bowler or he is not a bowler.

A. E. Knight
The Complete Cricketer (1906)

100. Probably a too easy delivery is not possible to the very greatest bowler, to one at once natural and cultivated, and without much being acquired and much originally given true greatness is not. There are many great bowlers, naturally gifted, but without thought and study they do not long endure at the highest level.

Ib.

101. Bowling which does not get men out, like batting which brings no runs to the score, is an art abused.

Ib.

102. Nevertheless, every one ought to bowl a little, if but to appreciate the anguish and the misery of indifferent fielding as a hard-working bowler knows it.

Ib.

103. The whole art of bowling is to make the batsman think that the ball is going to be of one kind when it is really of quite a different nature.

Sir Neville Cardus (quoting B. J. T. Bosanquet)
Cricket (1930)

104. There is a deal of head-work in bowling: once make your batsman set his mind on one hit, and give him a ball requiring the contrary, and he is off his guard in a moment.

James Pycroft
The Cricket Field (1851)

105. There is a final drop of venom which transforms a good bowler into a great one.

Hon. T. C. F. Prittie
Mainly Middlesex (1947)

106. The really great bowler knows more of the game than anyone else, or at least has opportunities of knowing it.

A. E. Knight
The Complete Cricketer (1906)

107. Of all members of the cricket family, the bowler is the supreme head. He is as the trunk from which even the greatest branches depend; he is the great soldier at the flank upon whom the goodly company wheels.

Ib.

108. The bowler, infinitely greater in finesse, in blend of brain and muscle, invites, as he needs, the co-operation of his ten comrades.

Ib.

109. The subtle finger touch of a great bowler often suffers by his grasping of the bat handle for any length of time, and a period of rest will assist him to recover.

Ib.

110. Bowling is a very delightful art, if you can play go-as-you please with it; but from the grim drudgery of its prolonged effort nine out of ten professionals shrink.

Ib.

111. I have noticed that a really good bowler appears in the ranks of the professionals about once in half-a-dozen years, and amongst the amateurs about once in twelve.

W. G. Grace
Cricket (1891)

112. It is better a thousand times to bowl an over-pitched ball than a short one at any time of his innings.

Ib.

113. It is an egregious error to suppose that every bowler has an equal facility of applying the same set of muscles when in play, with the certainty of achieving that object for accomplishment of which by another, his envious or emulating feeling has been aroused. The mere act of delivering the ball *before*, or of retaining it an instant *after* the hand has arrived at a given point, will make all the difference.

William Denison
Sketches of the Players (1846)

114. The fault I find with many bowlers of the present day is that the ball comes from their hands too often like a bit of lead. It ought to come as if it had a fiend inside it, which works the mischief immediately it touches the ground.

A. W. Pullin (quoting Buchanan)
Talks with Old English Cricketers (1900)

115. It is usually, and, I think, with reason regarded as a sign of a bowler's decline when his action becomes lower.

K. S. Ranjitsinhji
The Jubilee Book of Cricket (1897)

116. Between the bowler who not only is master of his art but knows how to apply it, who is thinking hard all the time he is bowling, who is trying to get the batsman out every ball he bowls, and the bowler who in a mechanical, non-thinking manner sends down ball after ball with no definite intention, and without any reference to what the wicket is and who the batsman, the difference is the same, in due proportion, as that between a Napoleon and a Xerxes.

Ib.

117. A school eleven, as indeed every other, only requires four regular bowlers. 'If you cannot win with four bowlers, you'll never win at all' is an old and true saying.

A. G. Steel
The Badminton Library – Cricket (1904)

118. Give me the bowler whose fingers, embracing me,
Tingle and throb with the joy of the game,
One who can laugh at a smack to the boundary,
Single of purpose and steady of aim.

E. V. Lucas
The Cricket Ball Sings (1899)

119. The bowler is a more delicate plant, less certain to rear, and shorter-lived than the batsman.

I. A. R. Peebles
Talking of Cricket (1953)

120. Bowlers tend to become cricketing heroes for what they do as distinct from how they do it.

J. M. Kilburn
Overthrows (1975)

121. A great bowler has physical power, determination, co-ordination and some special gift, usually pace from the pitch, which makes him dangerous to begin with.

C. L. R. James
Beyond a Boundary (1963)

122. When a master bowler lacks support, his opponents can regard him as a problem separate from the remainder of his team's outcricket.

John Arlott
Maurice Tate (1951)

123. Every ball that he bowled had brain behind it, if not exactness of pitch.

A. G. Macdonell
England, Their England (1933)

124. Let not the young cricketer attempt the very fast bowling, unless he be gifted with those capabilities by the hand of nature which entitle him to assume it.

William Denison
Sketches of the Players (1846)

125. A fast bowler must be straight to be good.

A. G. Steel
The Badminton Library – Cricket (1904)

126. Fast bowlers depend on their pace and length to beat the batsmen.

W. G. Grace
Cricket (1891)

127. Fast bowling combines brute strength, suppleness, rhythm and timing – you have to have a measure of each.

Peter Walker
The All-Rounder (1979)

128. A large physique is an encouragement – almost a mandate – to bowl as fast as one can.

David Frith
The Fast Men (1975)

129. A long run is likely to cause the batsman's attention and vigilance to flag, and tends to breed uncertainty in his mind; adds sting and force to bowling; gives the bowler time to make up his mind what to bowl; and contributes largely, if properly managed, to the deceptiveness of a variation of pace.

K. S. Ranjitsinhji
The Jubilee Book of Cricket (1897)

130. Fast bowlers, on the other hand, depend in the first instance upon sheer pace to get wickets.

Ib.

131. Genuinely fast bowling, too, finds out batsmen short of the highest class because their reactions are not quick enough to deal with it.

John Arlott
An Eye for Cricket (1979)

132. I have never known many professionals who relished it, because, as their bread-and-butter depends on their playing, they naturally do not want to be knocked about.

Lord Hawke (of fast bowling)
Recollections and Reminiscences (1924)

133. Even the best swerver, however, is dependent on a number of elements beyond his control, such as the state of the ball, the humidity of the atmosphere, and the greenness of the pitch.

I. A. R. Peebles
Talking of Cricket (1953)

134. Persistence, muscle, luck and, of course, some skill, make up the average seam bowler.

A. V. Bedser
Over and Out in *The Cricketer's Bedside Book* (1966)

135. It used to be a maxim of the game that your fast bowler was not to be considered as bowling well *until* he had been punched a time or two through the covers for four.

E. H. D. Sewell
Well Hit! Sir (1947)

136. No batsman likes the bouncer, not even an occasional one, no more than he would like a sticky wicket, but there is nothing in the laws of cricket to prevent the bowler pitching one short if he so desires. I would go so far as to say that the fast bowler is entitled to let one go every now and again, and providing it is not a deliberate or vindictive attack on the batsman himself I am sure no player worthy of the name would offer protest.

Leslie Ames
Close of Play (1953)

137. Body-line itself was no more lethal, or sustained an attack on the batsman's body than the more modern version practised by Lillee, Thomson and others, but it embittered relations to a remarkable degree and Jardine was the focus of hostility.

H. A. Pawson
Runs and Catches (1980)

138. Body-line was not an incident, it was not an accident, it was not a temporary aberration. It was the violence and ferocity of our age expressing itself in cricket.

C. L. R. James
Beyond a Boundary (1963)

139. Body-line bowling assumed such proportions as to menace best interests of game, making protection of body by batsmen the main consideration and causing intensely bitter feeling between players, as well as injury. In our opinion it is unsportsmanlike and unless stopped at once is likely to upset friendly relations existing between Australia and England.

Australian Board Cable to M.C.C. (1933)

140. Fast bowling, unlike slow, has not to trust to deceptive arts.

A. E. Knight
The Complete Cricketer (1906)

141. Shake off the fetish – it is little else – that you *must* begin with two fast, or fastish bowlers. That is no more than a bad habit, *unless* you have two really good fast ones who happen to be the two best bowlers in your team.

E. H. D. Sewell
Well Hit! Sir (1947)

142. There is real art in bowling opponents out or in getting them caught or stumped out by the clever pitching of a well-spun ball. There is none whatever in trying to frighten them out.

Ib.

143. The greatest slow bowlers, Rhodes, Blythe, Grimmett and Verity, have been the poker-players of the cricket field, disguising beneath a bland and perfectly simulated indifference the real depth and cunning of their designs.

Hon. T. C. F. Prittie
Mainly Middlesex (1947)

144. All the players, particularly those who have more recently come out, ridicule slow bowling as 'stuff', and talk largely before they go in, of what they will do with it – how they will hit it here, cut it there, and drive it forward – but what have they done against it when in?

William Denison
Sketches of the Players (1846)

145. There is something so tempting to an inexperienced player in seeing a ball chucked up in the air slowly and simply, it looks so very easy to hit, so peculiarly guileless, that a wild slog is frequently the result, too often followed by disastrous consequences.

A. G. Steel
The Badminton Library – Cricket (1904)

146. Leg-breakers have a fascination for those who, using what vehemence and accuracy they may, hurl through the strenuous day with little enough of spin or stratagem.

R. C. Robertson-Glasgow
Cricket Prints (1943)

147. Leg-break is artificial rather than natural, and is much more difficult to produce than off-break. Hence it is not surprising that exponents of it are rare, at least successful exponents.

K. S. Ranjitsinhji
The Jubilee Book of Cricket (1897)

148. Leg-spinners pose problems much like love,
Requiring commitment, the taking of a chance.

Alan Ross
Watching Benaud Bowl (1963)

149. And bowler, to you a caution or two,
To save your own side from disaster;
Don't mind if you're hit, tempt the batsmen a bit,
And vary your slows with a faster;
Keep him all in a fret as to what's coming yet,
For if he gets set he will trouble you –
And if (for his sins) you bowl at his shins
Don't shout for a mean l.b.w.

Anonymous
A Song of Cricket

150. I bowled three sanctified souls
With three consecutive balls!
What do I care if Blondin trod
Over Niagara Falls?
What do I care for the loon in the Pit
Or the gilded earl in the Stalls?
I bowled three curates once
With three consecutive balls.

Norman Gale
Cricket Songs (1890)

151. It is but justice to Dearman to say that he delighted the spectators
throughout by his unflinching bottom; and certainly no man could
have continued such a contest against such fearful odds, with more
good humour and unshaken pluck; his bowling never flagged from
first to last.

William Denison
Sketches of the Players (1846)

152. As with the bat so with the ball,
And bygone hours come back,
When he was honoured with the call
To open the attack:
Alas! this compliment is gone,
Captains and creeds are strange,
And all too rarely he goes on
Till sixth or seventh change.

Alfred Cochrane
Verba non Facta in *Later Verses* (1918)

Fielding

LORDS CRICKET GROUND. ETON & HARROW. 1895.

153. Collectively and individually fielding is largely a matter of thought and discipline.

I. A. R. Peebles
Talking of Cricket (1953)

154. Several players were stationed to 'look out', in different parts of the field, and each fixed himself into the proper attitude by placing one hand on each knee, and stooping very much as if he were 'making a back' for some beginner at leap-frog. All the regular players do this sort of thing; indeed it is generally supposed that it is quite impossible to look out in any other position.

Charles Dickens
Pickwick Papers (1837)

155. Everyone ought to have his fixed position in the field and stick to it.

Sir John Cecil Masterman
Fate Cannot Harm Me (1935)

156. Let me here mention another curious fact never published, namely, that the senior professional on the Yorkshire side always fielded at point.

Lord Hawke
Recollections and Reminiscences (1924)

157. Fielding is the only branch of the game in which, if one tries hard enough, one can be sure of success.

K. S. Ranjitsinhji
The Jubilee Book of Cricket (1897)

158. Always try for a catch, however impossible it may seem.

Ib.

159. Quite possibly you may practise batting and bowling for many a day, and the only thing noticeable about you as a result of it all will be your enthusiasm. Make the same indefatigable effort to improve your fielding, and the gods cannot stop you.

A. E. Knight
The Complete Cricketer (1906)

160. Fielding is a double-edged weapon. Smart work, especially the snapping up of those half-chance catches, has a detrimental effect on the batsmen, but at the same time it puts the bowler's tail up. I have always maintained that although every player cannot be an all-rounder in the fullest sense of the term, there is no reason at all why all cricketers should not be able to hold their own in the field.

Leslie Ames
Close of Play (1953)

161. It is surprising that the famous nurseries of amateur cricket, the great English Public Schools, with all their advantages, so rarely produce fielders of more than average ability.

K. S. Ranjitsinhji
The Jubilee Book of Cricket (1897)

162. A bad field is an eyesore to spectators and a millstone round the neck of his side. Out upon him for a nuisance to society!

Ib.

163. It is a disgrace. It shows an execrable attitude of the mind. A slack, careless fielder needs the stick: he cannot possibly have a right and proper spirit.

Ib.

164. Mid-on is perhaps the best place to put a duffer, if you are unfortunate enough to have one on your side. He will do less harm there than anywhere else.

Ib.

165. Mid-on is one of the easiest places in the field; for there is no twist on the ball, and the fieldsman has plenty of time to see it coming to him.

W. G. Grace
Cricket (1891)

166. On the whole, I think the easiest position in the field, and the one to which I should give the duffer his place, is mid-on, for though the ball may come quickly to that fieldsman, it generally comes straight from the bat.

W. G. Grace
W.G. – Cricketing Reminiscences and Personal Recollections (1899)

167. A captain of an eleven feels himself very often bound by an unwritten tradition to put the notoriously worst field in his eleven short-leg.

Hon. R. H. Lyttleton
The Badminton Library – Cricket (1904)

168. The old days had their stars; they also had their leisurely, portly gentlemen, such as Percy Perrin who, when asked if he had really stopped one of Hobbs' boundaries down Vauxhall way, replied reasonably: 'Oh, yes. Mind you, they ran eight.'

A. A. Thomson
Were the Old Ones so Good? in *The Cricketer's Bedside Book* (1966)

169. It may be taken as true that a bad fielding school eleven denotes a bad and slack captain.

A. G. Steel
The Badminton Library – Cricket (1904)

170. Many and many a promising match has been lost by bad management in the Field; not because the Fieldsmen were not well qualified, young, quick, and full of life and activity – but from a want of making a just estimate of the powers of the Batsman, and thereby leaving positions open to one which ought to be chosen for another; and these positions again being subject to change, according to the pace of the bowling.

Nicholas Wanostrocht
Felix on the Bat (1845)

71. A bowler should never grumble aloud at catches being missed; the unfortunate man has done his best and failed, and any censure only makes him more flurried and adds to his discomfiture without doing any good.

A. G. Steel
The Badminton Library – Cricket (1904)

72. As I once heard a sarcastic Scotchman say up at Selkirk, 'Macdonald is a good fielder, nothing can pass his feet.'

A. E. Knight
The Complete Cricketer (1906)

73. The crowd's dejected, the scorer scores,
And I'm expected to save the fours!

Herbert Farjeon
Long-on Blues in Cricket Bag (1946)

74. The sun in the heavens was beaming;
The breeze bore an odour of hay,
My flannels were spotless and gleaming,
My heart was unclouded and gay;
The ladies, all gaily apparelled,
Sat round looking on at the match,
In the tree-tops the dicky-birds carolled,
All was peace till I bungled that catch.

P. G. Wodehouse
Missed!

75. Stupendous scores he never made,
But perished ever with despatch:
No bowling genius he displayed,
But once, in a forgotten match,
He made a catch.

Alfred Cochrane
The Catch in Collected Verses (1903)

76. The quivering poise! the dart!
The wristy, magical, and stern
Completeness of that punishing Return.

Norman Gale
Back Numbers!

177. He leaps once more, with eager spring,
     To catch the brief-glimpsed, flying ball
     And quickens to its sudden sting:

John Arlott
The Old Cricketer

178. Sunburned fieldsmen, flannelled dream,
     Looked, though urgent, scarce alive,
     Swooped, like swallows of a cream
     On skimming fly, the hard-hit drive.

John Arlott
Cricket at Worcester, 1938

179. Had I but youth, keen-sighted I would lour
     To track the flying ball, on fleet foot scour
     The field all day to save the quick-snatched run
     And feel, how good they were, when sets the sun,
          Those hours of Life!

D. L. A. Jephson
Had I But Youth in *A Few Overs* (1913)

180. Defeat was certain, and he had been bowling all through a long
     innings, but a run had been saved, and it seemed to him well worth
     while.

Hugh Vibart Macnaghten
Fifty Years of Eton (1924)

181. He seemed to possess a kind of telescopic arm and hand, which
     would shoot out and reach the apparently impossible.

A. E. Knight (of Carpenter)
The Complete Cricketer (1906)

182. Fielding in the so-called 'silly' positions, after all, is not merely an
     act of courage which deserves applause when it is truly that and not
     a half-hearted pretence. It is also an intimidation of the batsman, an
     emotional pressure which can only be justified if the fieldsmen are
     prepared to yield their own security in return, and as much of a
     distraction as the presence of a spectator alongside the grandmaster's
     chess-board. The use of an artificial aid to increase the already heavy
     odds in favour of the bowling side and against the solitary bat is to
     tip the fine balance between what is fair play and what is not.

Geoffrey Moorhouse
The Best-Loved Game (1979)

183. As a general rule, I think it's stupid for a safe batsman or a good
bowler to put on the wicket-keeping gloves, as sooner or later he is
certain to get his hands damaged.

W. G. Grace
W.G. – Cricketing Reminiscences and Personal Recollections (1899)

184. When a fielder begins to be uncertain, he should keep wicket to fast
bowling for a quarter of an hour a day, and field somewhere close in
for a week or so.

Hon. R. H. Lyttleton
The Badminton Library – Cricket (1904)

185. Now the wicket-keeper's connection with the bowler is closest of
all. It is as if the bowler were at one end of a telegraph wire and the
wicket-keeper at the other.

K. S. Ranjitsinhji
The Jubilee Book of Cricket (1897)

186. Personally, I should like to see the wicket-keeper more handsomely
rewarded than he is, and I would infringe upon the delightful social
communism of our fees to the extent of awarding him an extra
sovereign in every match.

A. E. Knight
The Complete Cricketer (1906)

187. It is impossible to estimate too highly the qualities that make up a
good wicket-keeper. It demands the quickest of eye, the staunchest
of nerve, the steadiest of purpose, the most unflinching of
resolution.

'Quid'
Jerks in from Short Leg (1866)

188. The Wicket-Keeper
He therefore is the General, and is deputed to direct all the
movements of the fieldsmen: not, however, by word of command,
like the military commander, but by the simple motion of his hand;
and the reason for this will be obvious to every one; for instead of
calling out to each fieldsman distinctly, and by so doing putting the
striker upon his guard, the alteration and exact position of each
fieldsman is effected in perfect silence.

John Nyren
The Young Cricketer's Tutor (1833)

H. R. Butt (1865–1928).

89. The position of the wicket-keeper in his standing should be that of a man preparing to spar, so that he may in an instant move any way he pleases.

Ib.

90. Many wicket-keepers will frequently put down the wicket when the striker has not moved from his ground; but this practice is doubly objectionable in the eyes of a good cricketer, and is after all but a piece of stage effect, and to make a show.

Ib.

91. The wicket-keeper also is not allowed to annoy the striker, either by noise, uncalled-for-remarks, or unnecessary action.

Ib.

92. Wicket-keeping is an art, the skilful wicket-keeper an artist. It is as great a distinction to be a wicket-keeper in cricket as it is to be a Hardy in fiction.

'Blazer'
Some Cover Shots (1924)

93. The wicket-keeper in an average cricket team is often regarded as a player who fulfils his duties simply because he is in love with them, and because, as we are led to assume, they are as natural to him as the instinct we find in a cow for chewing part of an adjacent meadow.

Ib.

94. Stumping requires, above all, speed of hand and eye. Speed of foot is complementary but subsidiary. For, generally speaking, the first-class batsman leaves his ground for so short a time that it is barely possible to stump him off the widish ball, which requires more than the movement of a single foot to reach.

Hon. T. C. F. Prittie
Mainly Middlesex (1947)

95. Wicket-keeping then was a painful business with thin gloves and no inner glove. That explains the advice received from England's leading keeper, Herbert Strudwick. When my father asked him for hints on technique, he was startled by the reply, 'You must rinse your hands in the chamber-pot every day. The urine hardens them wonderfully.'

H. A. Pawson
Runs and Catches (1980)

Captaincy
and Committee

It is important for all captains to think about the crowd which has paid to watch.

196. The chief qualifications for a good captain are a sound knowledge of the game, a calm judgment, and the ability to inspire others with confidence.

A. G. Steel
The Badminton Library – Cricket (1904)

197. No captain who wins the toss and puts the other side in deserves to win the match, unless there are some very exceptional circumstances to be taken into his consideration.

Ib.

198. Murdoch, of course, had a thoroughly sound knowledge of the game; but his better judgment was too frequently hampered by the ceaseless chattering and advice of one or two men who never could grasp the fact that in the cricket-field there can only be one captain.

Ib.

199. It is a strange fact connected with cricket that a good captain is but seldom met with.

Ib.

200. An organism must have a central principle to make it efficient, and a captain ought to be this central principle to his side.

K. S. Ranjitsinhji
The Jubilee Book of Cricket (1897)

201. The captain creates the moral atmosphere of his side. If he is slack and indifferent, so are the other ten; if he is keen and enthusiastic, so are they. Unconsciously, the side as a whole assumes the captain's attitude towards cricket and towards a particular match.

Ib.

202. A good captain tries to identify himself so completely with his side, as a whole and in all its parts, that he fields with every fieldsman and bowls every ball with his bowlers. He is, in truth, the soul of his side.

Ib.

203. And to be a good captain, a man must first of all have the natural gift for leadership – which is probably an inborn quality synonymous with force of character – and then be able to apply this gift to the requirements of cricket.

Ib.

204. Roger: I'm the captain. It's me who controls whether we win or lose and I want to win, Mim, no point else. There's this very fine balance. It's all psychology. Which means tact and diplomacy.

Richard Harris
Outside Edge (Act One) (1979)

205. Cricket depends more almost than any other game on the quality of leadership, and the difficulty today of happening on the right man where several probably are of similar seniority and background is one of its most pressing problems.

E. W. Swanton
Sort of a Cricket Person (1972)

206. Cricket has become so scientific that a captain of today has to work hard. Gone are the days when a captain could change the bowling by the clock or set the field in the same position for every batsman.

> Sir Pelham Warner
> *Long Innings* (1951)

207. A captain must always make his decision *before* he knows what will happen. The critic usually bases his statements on what *has* happened and thus takes no risk.

> Sir Donald Bradman
> *Farewell to Cricket* (1950)

208. Every manoeuvre must be tried in a desperate state of the game; but, above all things, be slow and steady, being also especially careful that your field do not become confused. Endeavour by every means in your power – such as, by changing the bowling, by little alterations in the field, or by any excuse you can invent, to delay the time, that the strikers may become cold and inactive. And when you get a turn in your favour, you may push on the game a little faster; but even then be not too flushed with success, but let your play be still cool, cautious, and steady.

> John Nyren
> *The Young Cricketer's Tutor* (1833)

209. A captain's most important job is on the field. Watch your fieldsmen like a hawk.

> H. M. Herman
> *How's That?* (1937)

210. The next man in was Barrie (Capt.). On returning he received an ovation.

> Sir J. M. Barrie
> *Allahakbarries C.C.* (1899)

211. A captain is, then, not only perfectly justified, but is bound in the interests of his side, and in the true interests of the game, to order his men to get out if that is the only way to win.

> A. G. Steel
> *The Badminton Library – Cricket* (1904)

Sir C. Aubrey Smith (1863–1948).

212. At one point on the second day, with the Australian attack beginning to take a hammering, Christofani limped off the field with a 'strained groin muscle'. He didn't reappear until half an hour before stumps when he suddenly raced on to the field, heading towards the spot where the substitute 12th man had been fielding. Hassett however must have suspected that his bowler had been taking an unnecessary 'rest'. For with elaborate hand signals like a policeman in charge of the traffic, he began directing him to a new position. Christofani with a worried look on his face couldn't make out exactly where he was meant to stand. To the right. To the left. A little more. Now back. The crowd was equally mystified. But Hassett's intentions eventually became plain as the fieldsman was worked into a position opposite the gate, then back, back, through the gate and off the field.

> Edward Docker
> *History of Indian Cricket* (1976)

213. No matter how genial he may be, a captain must command respect; he must at all times be dignified; indeed, his success is due in great measure to the fact that he is different from the majority of his fellow-cricketers.

> M. A. Noble
> *The Game's The Thing* (1926)

214. A captain who makes no allowance for mistakes and is for ever grumbling discourages effort and honest endeavour.

> Ib.

215. I believe that in first-class cricket it is important for all captains to think more than some do about the crowd which has paid to watch.

> Sir Leonard Hutton
> *Just My Story* (1956)

216. Cricket teams have often suffered from captains who have arrived, done queer things, departed and been forgotten.

> R. C. Robertson-Glasgow
> *Cricket Prints* (1943)

217. Teams are far too critical of captains.

> A. E. Knight
> *The Complete Cricketer* (1906)

218. Pray God, no professional shall ever captain England. I love and admire them all but we have always had an amateur skipper and when the day comes when we shall have no more amateurs captaining England it will be a thousand pities.

Lord Hawke, Reply to Vote of
Thanks at Yorkshire A.G.M. (1925)

219. A Selector's job is interesting, sometimes exasperating, occasionally heartbreaking.

Sir Donald Bradman
Farewell to Cricket (1950)

220. Captaincy by committee on or off the field is lamentable.

A. E. Knight
The Complete Cricketer (1906)

221. But it is important for a captain to feel that he has the Committee behind him and that they leave it to him to run the game on the field. Sometimes members of committees are not very experienced cricketers themselves, and they are not always right in their view of what goes on during play. There is a tremendously important job to be done by committees with regard to finance, the running of the ground and so on, but they should leave the conduct of the game itself to the captain. Otherwise they unsettle him and unsettle the side.

R. E. S. Wyatt
Three Straight Sticks (1951)

222. Selection committees are useful institutions, because discussion often throws new light upon things, comparisons of opinion frequently extract the truth, and in many ways several heads are better than one.

K. S. Ranjitsinhji
The Jubilee Book of Cricket (1897)

223. I recall that J. A. Dixon, the Nottingham captain, condoled with me about this, and said, 'It takes a long time to become recognised in big cricket, and just as long to be dropped from it.'

C. B. Fry
Life Worth Living (1939)

Umpires

THE UMPIRE.
WILLIAM CALDERCOURT born at Blisworth in 1802.

224. The umpire is the law of cricket personified, image of the noble constitution of the best of games.

Sir Neville Cardus
Good Days (1934)

225. The umpire at cricket is like the geyser in the bath-room; we cannot do without it, yet we notice it only when it is out of order.

Ib.

226. Really exact and eager umpiring puts a razor edge on players' keenness. One faulty decision may ruin not only a match but somebody's form for a month.

W. J. Edrich
Cricket Heritage (1948)

227. An umpire should be a man – they are, for the most part, old women – and he should have had a thorough practical initiation into the mysteries of the game.

'Quid'
Jerks in from Short Leg (1866)

228. In no department of the game has so little progress been made as in that which is summed up in the little word 'umpire'.

Ib.

229. The country umpire is a sensitive animal, and is prone to believe upon being asked several ridiculous questions that he is the object of chaff, and he may for that reason retaliate in a manner very unsatisfactory to the gentlemen cutting the chaff.

Ib.

230. Umpires are very peculiar individuals; once let it enter their heads that a bowler is trying to 'jockey' a decision out of them, up go their backs, and they suddenly become a mechanical toy that glibly answers every appeal with the two words 'Not out,' and those only.

A. G. Steel
The Badminton Library – Cricket (1904)

231. If anyone were to ask us the question 'What class of useful men receive most abuse and least thanks for their service?' we should, without hesitation, reply, 'Cricket umpires'.

Ib.

232. It is an absolute impossibility to find an umpire who will not make mistakes at times.

Ib.

233. The problem of unsatisfactory umpiring will doubtless persist until we have all reached a Nirvana where the fever of desire is unknown. Until that day dawn, we can certainly make cricket a more sweet and pleasant game by minimising our absurd appeals, and by accepting in the kindliest fashion the decrees of these interpreters of the law, appropriately named umpires.

A. E. Knight
The Complete Cricketer (1906)

234. Umpires need to be helped and encouraged in all countries – for they are an integral part of the game. The greater the importance of the match, the more quickly can an error upset the balance of power.

Sir Donald Bradman
Farewell to Cricket (1950)

235. English umpires, generally speaking, are better than Australians.

Ib.

236. I attribute the friction which has frequently arisen during the visits of English teams to Australia to the fact that even at the present time Australia is not well provided with good umpires.

W. G. Grace
W.G. – Cricketing Reminiscences and Personal Recollections (1899)

237. Whether it is a spontaneous outburst of pent-up nervous energy or a tactical weapon, the mass team appeal is nevertheless a completely new phenomenon in the first-class game.

John Arlott
An Eye for Cricket (1979)

238. The extent of strain can be measured by the retirement of some of the best Australian and West Indian umpires.

Ib.

239. I must avoid that umpire, too.
One ball, I'm pretty sure,
That hits my bat before my leg
And he'll give me leg-before.

A. M. Robertson
The Cricket Match

240. That he was 'in' the batsman never doubted
Delighted he'd escaped the dreaded 'blob' –
When suddenly 'How's that?' was loudly shouted;
The umpire answered, 'Out! I *wins five bob!*'

W. N. Cobbold
A Village Cricket Match

241. His devotion to the game of cricket was rewarded when he achieved
an eminence and reputation as an umpire quite unprecedented and
still unrivalled. For many years the keenness of his senses, his power
of sustained concentration, and his profound knowledge made him
a seemingly infallible judge of any cricket situation.

Diana Rait Kerr and I. A. R. Peebles (of Frank Chester)
Lord's 1946–1970 (1971)

242. Personally, I am against umpires lying on pavements – on the
grounds of inconvenience to pedestrians and because it could set an
embarrassing precedent.

Michael Melford
A Rummy Affair in Bombay in *The Cricketer's Bedside Book* (1966)

Wickets,
Places and Tests

*There was never a
better way of watching
cricket than at Lord's.*

ENGLAND IN 1842: A CRICKET MATCH AT LORD'S.

243. Somewhere it has been written that the cultured man of money can
best use it by keeping a string quartet and commissioning a first-
class yacht. To this should be added the creation of a pretty well-
appointed cricket ground.

Tom Watson
Ibis Cricket, 1870–1949 (1950)

244. This is without question the most beautiful cricket ground in the
world.

Sir Donald Bradman (of Brockton Point Ground, Vancouver)
Farewell to Cricket (1950)

45. In every school there is a sacred place
More holy than the chapel. Ours was yours:
I mean, of course, the first eleven pitch.
Here in the welcome break from morning work,
The heavier boys, of milk and biscuits full,
Sat on the roller while we others pushed
Its weighty cargo slowly up and down.
We searched the grass for weeds, caressed the turf,
Lay on our stomachs squinting down its length
To see that all was absolutely smooth.

Sir John Betjeman
Cricket Master

46. O yes, I love that bit of greensward there!
For on it I forget my worldly care
When two opposing parties, with a will,
Join to display and test each other's skill.

William Bange
Fair Grove in *The Happy Village and other poems* (1848)

47. Lord's and the Oval truly mean
Zenith of hard-won fame,
But it was just a village green
Mothered and made the game.

G. D. Martineau
The Village Pitch

48. Real old-fashioned village cricket is a serious matter for the villager
and immense fun for the visitor.

I. A. R. Peebles
Talking of Cricket (1953)

49. I know of nothing more painful in this world than to see some of
our Saturday afternoon local cricket games.

A. E. Knight
The Complete Cricketer (1906)

250. Amidst thy bowers the tyrant's hand is seen,
The rude pavilions sadden all thy green;
One selfish pastime grasps the whole domain,
And half a faction swallows up the plain;
Adown thy glades, all sanctified to cricket,
The hollow-sounding bat now guards the wicket;

Lewis Carroll
The Deserted Parks (1867)

251. Country-house cricket reminds one of days spent in eating apples under an old tree, reading the *Earthly Paradise* of William Morris.

A. E. Knight
The Complete Cricketer (1906)

252. By its nature and constituents a Cricket Week is an institution peculiarly English, for it connotes the very essence and quiddity of an English countryside in summer and the deep-rooted democratic devotion to a national game which eliminates all mere social and intellectual distinctions.

Lt.-Col. C. P. Hawkes
Bat, Ball and Buskin in *The Times*, 25 May 1937 and *M.C.C.,
1787–1937* (1937)

253. In no other country but England would the attack and defence of three stumps be witnessed by enormous crowds of fashionable people with unflagging zest, and there are not many foreigners as yet who would care to face a swift bowler with no other protection than a bat.

Charles Box
The English Game of Cricket (1877)

254. I'm not at all surprised the French have never understood this game, whose players cannot be *serieux* when their honour is at stake.

Geoffrey Moorhouse
The Best-Loved Game (1979)

255. It is a brave pastime, a game for soldiers, for each tries to strike the other with the ball, and it is but a small stick with which you ward it off. Three sticks behind show the spot beyond which you may not retreat. I can tell you that it is no game for children, and I will confess that, in spite of my nine campaigns, I felt myself turn pale when the first ball floated past me.

Sir Arthur Conan Doyle
Adventures of Gerard (1903)

256. To stand upright during so many hours of an extreme heat; to take a violent exercise without any need; to run deliberately a grave danger not less than that which one is obliged to encounter on a field of battle – all this is folly of the most profound. I cannot believe that there is really some pleasure at all in it. You English are eccentric; and the verity of it is that you play cricket because in playing it you show yourselves different from all the rest of the world.

Anatole Gonjon (1884) quoted in
In Celebration of Cricket (1978)

257. The name 'cricket' practically defies translation and wherever it is played today it is played under the original English name.

P. G. G. Labouchere, T. A. J. Provis and Peter S. Hargreaves
The Story of Continental Cricket (1969)

258. It's remarkable how great a grip cricket's got over so many parts of the Commonwealth, and not merely on people of European stock. I can't help thinking that there's some connection between a liking for democratic ideals and the game of cricket. Both require patience, tolerance and understanding. Both are not as spectacular as many other forms of government or forms of games, and are only appreciated when their finer points are grasped.

R. E. S. Wyatt
Three Straight Sticks (1951)

259. But international cricket matches are not only cricket matches. They tend as well to excite and promote a kindly feeling between the nations which take part in them.

Bishop Welldon
Introduction to *How We Recovered the Ashes* (1904)

260. It is not uncommon, to this day, for touring sides to be hailed as heroes on arrival, and dismissed as nobodies when things go wrong.

Alan Gibson
The Cricket Captains of England (1979)

261. Armstrong's circus provided rare entertainment, its ring-master provoked much abuse.

Kenneth Gregory
In Celebration of Cricket (1978)

262. I always think that the intense interest which nowadays is evinced in the matches between England and Australia began with the tour of Stoddart's team in Australia during the winter of 1894–95.

Sir Pelham Warner
Lord's 1787–1945 (1946)

263. The Australian climate is a great aid to bowling and fielding. Its warmth and mildness prevent the rheumatic affections that so often attack the arms and shoulders of our players, and the Australians consequently retain their suppleness of limb and activity of youth longer than their English cousins.

A. G. Steel
The Badminton Library – Cricket (1904)

264. When the Australians come to England people here tend to lose their sense of proportion about the game.

Margaret Hughes
All on a Summer's Day (1953)

265. I admire the Australians' approach to the game; they have the utmost ability for producing that little extra, or instilling into the opposition an inferiority complex that can have, and has had a crushing effect. Australians have no inhibitions.

Sir Leonard Hutton
Just My Story (1956)

266. Cricket in Australia demands quicker reflexes simply because everything, by which I principally mean the pace of the ball from hand to batsman or from bat to fieldsman, happens so much more swiftly than in England.

Ib.

267. The high road to greatness for an Australian is assiduous practice, for by that means he may achieve perfect stroke play, and after that the learning of versatility is easy by comparison with the reverse process. An Englishman has to learn versatility first, for otherwise he will not have sufficient opportunities to achieve perfection in his stroke play or in his technique.

P. G. H. Fender
County Cricket in *The Times*, 25 May 1937 and *M.C.C., 1787–1937*
(1937)

268. It struck me then, and I verified it later in other places, how notably higher the performance of average Australian cricketers was, age for age, than that of their English equivalents.

Sir Arthur Grimble
A Pattern of Islands (1952)

269. The Australian temper is at bottom grim; it is as though hot sun has dried up nature.

Sir Neville Cardus
Good Days (1934)

270. The Australian plays cricket to win; he has usually left it to Mr Warner to make Empire-binding speeches.

Ib.

271. Australians are notorious gamblers, and it probably has been an urge for adventure, combined with a natural partiality and prowess for attack, that lies at the core of the Australian way of cricket.

R. S. Whitington
An Illustrated History of Australian Cricket (1972)

272. Equally, the Australians, throughout cricket history, have been quick to strike back even from a position of apparently imminent defeat.

John Arlott
An Eye for Cricket (1979)

273. To play first-class cricket is a goal, and to reach the Australian XI, probably a higher honour than to go to England in the strict practical sense. But for many reasons it is a tour of England upon which most youngsters set their hearts.

Sir Donald Bradman
Farewell to Cricket (1950)

274. Next to representing England in a Test match at home, it is the highest ambition of every cricketer to be selected to go on tour to Australia.

Lord Hawke
Recollections and Reminiscences (1924)

275. If you are to be a Test Cricketer, you must also make an early and wise decision about demeanour and behaviour. Remember that nowadays the television camera may be trained on you when you least expect it.

R. C. Robertson-Glasgow
How to Become a Test Cricketer (1962)

276. Test Cricket is not a light-hearted business, especially that between England and Australia.

Sir Donald Bradman
Farewell to Cricket (1950)

277. Australians will not tolerate class distinction in sport.

J. H. Fingleton
Cricket Crisis (1946)

278. In any case, the only sane view of the amateur or professional question is the Australian one – 'Call us what you something well like but we want half the gate.'

J. C. Clay
Glamorgan County Cricket Club Year Book (1938)

279. Unconsciously, and perhaps without any suspicion on their part that such is the case, the Australians have seriously and perceptibly aggravated the symptoms of a commercial spirit in cricket.

James Lillywhite's Cricketers' Annual (1883)

280. The Australians came down like wolf on the fold,
The Marylebone Club for a trifle were bowled,
Our Grace before dinner was very soon done,
And Grace after dinner did not get a run.

Punch (June 1878)

281. Well done, Cornstalks, whipt us
    Fair and square.
Was it lucked that tripped us?
    Was it scare?
Kangaroo land's 'Demon', or our own
Want of devil, coolness, nerve, backbone?

Punch (August 1882)

282.
In Affectionate Remembrance
of
ENGLISH CRICKET
which died at The Oval
on
29th August, 1882
Deeply lamented by a large circle of
Sorrowing Friends and Acquaintances
R.I.P.
N.B. – The body will be cremated and
the Ashes taken to Australia
Sporting Times (September 1882)

283. When you have just lost the Ashes is no time to pick a bone with
the opposing spectators.
Alan Gibson
The Cricket Captains of England (1979)

284. Outside my own country I have played Test cricket in Australia,
New Zealand, India, Pakistan, the West Indies and South Africa.
Nowhere, not on any ground, have I experienced the thrill, the
inward thump that occurs before the first ball is bowled on the first
morning of a test at Lord's between England and Australia.
Ted Dexter and Clifford Makins
Testkill (1976)

285. Gone for ever are the days when we and Australia thought that we
were the only people who could really play cricket!
Sir Pelham Warner
Long Innings (1951)

286. Dick-a-Dick appeared to claim the largest share of individual
attention by 'dodging the ball'. Possessed of a narrow shield and
triangle, he defended himself against a shower of balls incessantly
pelting him from a distance of about twenty yards. He fenced off
many, that must have struck his head and other parts of the body,
with a wonderful adroitness by means of these primitive
instruments, while others he avoided by a leap or bound.
Charles Box
The English Game of Cricket (1877)

287. As a commercial speculation, the Black Team did not pay, but they played cricket against odds, and they often came out of the contest with honours.

Ib.

288. May 1676

6. This morning early (as it is custom all summer longe) at least 40 of the English, with his worship the Consull, rod out of the cytty about 4 miles to the Greene Platt, a fine vally by a river syde, to recreate them selves. Where a princely tent was pitched: and wee had severall pastimes and sports, as duck-hunting, fishing, shooting, hand-ball, krickett, scrofilo; and then a noble dinner brought thither, with greate plenty of all sorts of wine, punch, and lemonads; and at 6 wee returne all home in good order, but soundly tyred and weary.

The Diary of Henry Teonge, Chaplain on Board His Majesty's Ships *Assistance*, *Bristol*, and *Royal Oak*, Anno 1675 to 1679 (1825)

289. 'There are no snakes in Iceland.' The fastidious cricketer and the cynic are fain to paraphrase this exhaustive disquisition when the possibility of cricket in India is brought to their notice. But in India, as elsewhere, there is cricket 'of sorts'.

Captain Philip Trevor
The Lighter Side of Cricket (1901)

290. I fear it is only the violent enthusiast who can, generally speaking, enjoy cricket in India.

Ib.

291. It is urged, in general, that for Europeans cricket is not a game best suited to the conditions of modern India. It is, to begin with, too long a game. You want, in India, a game which is both violent and short.

Cecil Headlam
Ten Thousand Miles Through India and Burma (1903)

292. I saw a Parsi named Writer bowl against the Presidency Eleven and against Lord Hawke's Eleven, and considered at the time that for a few overs he was quite as difficult as that distinguished Nottingham bowler, George Wootton, and the action was extremely similar; but he could not keep it up as an English professional does, and it is in the matter of patience that I think the Indian will never be equal to the Englishman.

Lord Harris
A Few Short Runs (1921)

293. I am thankful to be able to feel sure that England has done much, very much, for India; and one of the many good things she has done has been to introduce a manly game which is open to poor as well as rich, which needs no prize beyond honour, and by its simple merits can enlist the support and countenance of the wisest men of each religion and caste.

Lord Harris (of Indian cricket)
Cricket (1925)

294. But India has an infinite capacity to absorb punishment. Everything blows over in the end.

Edward Docker
History of Indian Cricket (1976)

295. It has been noticed before in Indian cricket that there is a tendency for those who might be expected to give a lead at certain vital times to slip away into a kind of nether world where they cannot be held accountable. They render themselves *incommunicado*.

Ib.

296. In India team-selection has always been complicated by the many races, creeds and politics.

W. H. Brookes
Test Matches and Overseas Tours in *The Times*, 25 May 1937 and
M.C.C., 1787–1937 (1937)

297. The game called cricket is generally accepted as being as essential a part of the English landscape as the other great institution to be seen in that setting – the pub – and to almost any Englishman it would seem impossible that it could have its origin in any other surroundings.

P. G. G. Labouchere, T. A. J. Provis and Peter S. Hargreaves
The Story of Continental Cricket (1969)

298. The team left behind them an impression of keenness, combined with modesty and good humour.
> Sir Pelham Warner (of West Indian tourists, 1933)
> *Long Innings* (1951)

299. What do they know of cricket who only cricket know? West Indians crowding to Tests bring with them the whole past history and future hopes of the islands.
> C. L. R. James
> *Beyond a Boundary* (1963)

300. West Indian cricket has arrived at maturity because of two factors: the rise in the financial position of the coloured middle class and the high fees paid to players by the English leagues.
> Ib.

301. As clearly as if it was written across the sky, their play said: Here, on the cricket field if no-where else, all men in the island are equal, and we are the best men in the island. They had sting without the venom.
> (of Shannon C.C.)
> Ib.

302. The beginnings of cricket in the Pacific were not invariably attended by the spirit of brotherhood that this noble sport was once believed to inspire.
> Sir Arthur Grimble
> *A Pattern of Islands* (1952)

303. I take upon myself the credit of having shown the Australians how to prepare a wicket, and of disabusing their minds of the idea that a good wicket can be obtained without special care and preparation.
> W. G. Grace
> *W.G. – Cricketing Reminiscences and Personal Recollections* (1899)

304. The perfect wicket, moreover, compels a bowler to beat the batsman in the air rather than on the ground. Deceptiveness of flight and pace combined with qualities common to all good bowling stamps in unique fashion the great Australian bowler. To him brain must ever be the dominating factor in skill.
> A. E. Knight
> *The Complete Cricketer* (1906)

305. For in all places wickets are made for batsmen, and he must be indeed a great bowler who is uniformly successful upon them. Given but some measure of skill and a greater measure of patience, 'the great patience that outwearies fate', then may the batsman carry high hopes of fruition upon Australian wickets – if anywhere at all.

Ib.

306. Hard-wicket cricket is like chess – there is no element of chance in it, and only those who perfect themselves survive.

W. J. Edrich
Cricket Heritage (1948)

307. The day was warm and the wicket still so beautiful that the bowlers might well have watered it with tears.

Sir Neville Cardus
Good Days (1934)

308. My spirits are low and my scores are not high,
But day after day, we've soaked turf and grey sky,
And I shan't have a chance till the wickets get dry,
Oh willow, wet-willow, wet-willow!!!

Wet-Willow in *Mr Punch's Book of Sports*
edited by J. A. Hammerton (1906)

309. On a treacherous wicket all the batsman can do is to watch the ball with all his might and let the bat follow his eye.

K. S. Ranjitsinhji
The Jubilee Book of Cricket (1897)

310. Such words as 'dangerous', when applied to wickets, imply a normal man not of unique eyesight nor acrobatic celerity. They have no meaning to the genius who cuts from his eyebrows.

A. E. Knight
The Complete Cricketer (1906)

311. The wicket reminded me of a middle-aged gentleman's head of hair, when the middle-aged gentleman, to conceal the baldness of his crown, applies a pair of wet brushes to some favourite long locks and brushes them across the top of his head. So with the wicket.

Frederic Gale
Bell's Life, July 4 1868

312. It was clear that, after an apathetic youth and a hearty middle-age, the wicket was finishing its life in a mood of arthritic crotchetyness.

Denzil Batchelor
The Match I Remember (1950)

313. Hambledon cricket is a phenomenon within the history of the game.

John Arlott
Introduction to Nyren's *The Young Cricketer's Tutor* (1974)

314. At Hambledon cricket first reached maturity, through straight bat strokes, length bowling and highly organised fielding.

Ib.

315. Their cricket then seemed a mixture of the convivial, epic and idyllic.

Ib.

316. Games like cricket are not conceived and born like the mortals who play them. Nor if they give enjoyment are they allowed to perish; They are more likely to be adapted to suit the changing times. Having no traceable beginning, so they will have no sudden end.

Robin Marler
The Story of Cricket (1979)

317. Whatever great changes cricket may have undergone during the past century, it remained exactly as it is today in one respect – the start was delayed by rain.

Ben Travers
94 Declared (1981)

318. They were choice fellows, staunch and thorough-going. No thought of treachery ever seemed to have entered their heads. The modern politics of trickery and 'crossing' were (so far as my own experience and judgment of their actions extended) as yet 'a sealed book' to the Hambledonians; what they did, they did for love and honour of victory; and when (one who shall be nameless) sold the birthright of his good name for a mess of potage, he paid dearly for his bargain. It cost him the trouble of being a knave – (no trifle!); the esteem of his old friends, and, what was worst of all, the respect of him who could have been his *best* friend – himself.

John Nyren
The Young Cricketer's Tutor (1833)

319. There was high feasting held on Broad-Halfpenny during the solemnity of one of our grand matches. Oh! it was a heart-stirring sight to witness the multitude forming a complete and dense circle round the noble green. Half the county would be present, and all their hearts with us – Little Hambledon, pitted against all England was a proud thought for the Hampshire men. Defeat was glory in such a struggle – victory, indeed, made us only 'a little lower than angels'.

Ib.

320. Troy has fallen and Thebes is a ruin. The pride of Athens is decayed and Rome is crumbling to the dust. The philosophy of Bacon is wearing out and the victories of Marlborough have been overshadowed by greater laurels. All is vanity but cricket; all is sinking into oblivion but you. Greatest of all elevens, fare ye well!

Rev. John Mitford
Gentleman's Magazine (1833)

321. Bleak Broad-Halfpenny is now ploughed land; the slopes of Windmill Down glow yellow with corn, its summit given over to weed and copse.

A. E. Knight
The Complete Cricketer (1906)

322. Long, however, ere the cricket babe was rocked in the cradle of Hambledon, her little limbs had gathered strength upon the greens and commons of Surrey and Kent.

Ib.

323. One of the main objects of the county club should be, I take it, to stimulate the growth of cricket playing and the improvement of the standard of the game in every village.

Ib.

324. I love the old club, and anything I can do for it will make me happy.

Tom Watson
Ibis Cricket, 1870–1949 (1950)

325. Rule 6: That the Entrance be nothing, and the Annual Subscription do not exceed the entrance.

I Zingari Club (1857)

326. There is no doubt about the position of county cricket as a forcing house in the English game, for it offers to the individual player an opportunity for intensive practice of the game in competitive conditions, if he chooses so to regard his place in his county XI, and at the same time it offers him an almost day-to-day indulgence in one of the greatest pleasures possible to a cricketer, that of playing the game in good-class company to his heart's content.

P. G. H. Fender
County Cricket in *The Times*, 25 May 1937 and *M.C.C., 1787–1937*
(1937)

327. The Yorkshire hardness, attributed and cultivated, is a defensive quality expressed in the form of aggressiveness. It is resistance to challenge, unwillingness to bend the knee or doff the cap.

J. M. Kilburn
Overthrows (1975)

328. The Yorkshireman's intolerance of an enemy's prowess is simply the measure of the Yorkshireman's pride in his county's genius for cricket.

Sir Neville Cardus
Days in the Sun (1924)

329. Old Trafford, like Lancashire cricket, is both utilitarian and human.

Ib.

330. To use a venerable guide book term, the 'environs' of Old Trafford tend to lack aesthetic appeal, and normally fail to excite the imagination of the artist. Yet there is about Old Trafford an air, an unmistakable if intangible atmosphere of tolerant friendliness which is not fully dispelled, however desolate the climatic conditions or dastardly the intentions of invaders from across the Pennines or the world.

John Marshall
Old Trafford (1971)

331. This is the age of cruisers in the sky,
Of speed gone mad, of funerals in a hurry.
See to it then, that none of us shall die
Of tedium, Yorkshire, Lancashire and Surrey!

Norman Gale
A Point of View

332. Cricket, having been created and evolved, has achieved its purpose, produced one lovely thing, and ought to die.

C. P. Snow
Death Under Sail (1932)

333. The Oval is green,
Flats, gnats,
And white-clothed figures move with grace,
The bat and the ball!
These above all,
And the thrill, and the air of the place!

Leslie Frewin
*On Seeing Sir Learie Constantine Return (Temporarily) from Diplomacy
to Cricket* (1963)

334. It is delicious to read his own statement that he always preferred bowling on the Oval because there the wicket was perfect and he could regulate his breaks, while the rougher grounds were apt to upset his calculations.

H. S. Altham (of George Freeman)
A History of Cricket – Volume One (1926)

335. A fine day at the Oval makes us all akin, and a pleasant sight it is to see the vast assembly, every man with his eyes riveted on the wicket, every man able to appreciate the most delicate strokes in the game, and anxious to applaud friend or adversary.

Andrew Lang
Introduction to Richard Daft's *Kings of Cricket* (1893)

336. Wickets at the Oval were always much better than at Lord's, where the clay in the soil has always handicapped the ground men.

W. G. Grace
W.G. – Cricketing Reminiscences and Personal Recollections (1899)

337. At the Oval, men seem to have rushed away with some zest from their City offices. At Lord's there is a *dilettante* look, as of men whose work, if ever, has yet to come.

James Pycroft
Oxford Memories (1886)

338. But whatever change has taken place in cricket – or in me – I swear there is no change in the jolly Oval crowd. It is, as it has always been, the liveliest, most intense, most good-humoured mob that ever shouted itself hoarse at cricket. It is as different from the Lord's crowd as a country fair is from the Church Congress. At Lord's we take our cricket as solemnly as if we were at a prayer-meeting.

A. G. Gardiner
Many Furrows (1924)

339. The 'Mecca' of cricket must be
In the beautiful classic arena,
The home of the 'old' M.C.C.

Mr Punch's Book of Sports
edited by J. A. Hammerton (1906)

340. For cricket-lovers there is no place quite like Lord's during a Test match. Lord's must be a bit like Heaven. There are many mansions in it. It caters for all tastes, classes, colours, ages, points of view, degrees of skill, levels of knowledge.

T. C. Dodds
Hit Hard and Enjoy It (1976)

341. Lord's is a world apart. It is a community, an establishment, a living monument, an atmosphere.

Ib.

342. There was never a better way of watching cricket than at Lord's.

Eric Parker
Playing Fields (1922)

343. It is the best of all games, and I thank my stars that my early footsteps took me to Lord's, for, with all respect to the other great grounds, to me it is the best place in the world to play.

Denis Compton
Foreword to E. W. Swanton's *Denis Compton: A Cricket Sketch* (1948)

344. It is a wonderful feeling to walk from the pavilion out to the middle at Lord's for the first time. In recent years I have been on some of the biggest barrack squares in the country, but they have nothing on Lord's for vastness and when it comes to feeling lost.

Denis Compton
Playing for England (1948)

45. Yes, that ring at Lord's shows me every gradation in the scale of life
– the once active now stiff and heavy, the youthful grey, the leaders
of great elevens passing unrecognised and alone.

James Pycroft
Oxford Memories (1886)

46. Is there a more beautiful view in *England*, I wonder, than the view you
get from one of the stands in *Lord's* on a fine day? There is the
green and white of the field – as restful as a daisy field in *Chaucer*.
But there is also at *Lord's* a noble and multiple idleness that takes the
imagination, not to *Chaucer*, but to the *South Seas*.

Robert Lynd
The Sporting Life, and Other Trifles (1922)

47. Lord's – it's a magical word to me, the 'open sesame' to a lifetime of
happiness.

Margaret Hughes
All on a Summer's Day (1953)

48. It caught my youthful imagination, and from that day I have loved
every stick and stone of Lord's, and as the years pass I love it more
and more. Even now, after so many years, I feel something of a
thrill as I walk down St. John's Wood Road, and my heart, maybe,
beats a shade faster as I enter the ground.

Sir Pelham Warner
Long Innings (1951)

49. I always feel as though I am stepping into history.

J. M. Kilburn (of Lord's)
Overthrows (1975)

50. I know of nowhere else on earth where so much of cricket's flavour
is so readily concentrated.

Ib.

51. In the evening light Lord's is a place of infinite peace and quiet and
friendly charm.

Hon. T. C. F. Prittie
Mainly Middlesex (1947)

352. Lord's is still reckoned to be the greatest cricket ground in the world. The old Tavern has gone and its replacement is appalling enough; miniature skyscrapers disfigure the horizon as Central London steadily devours the village of St. John's Wood, but the ground has retained its sense of proportion and the superb Victorian pavilion (Architect, Mr. T. Verity) still subdues all innovations.
Ted Dexter and Clifford Makins
Testkill (1976)

353. 'Lord's' – that festival which the War had driven from the field – raised its light and dark blue flags for the second time, displaying almost every feature of a glorious past.
John Galsworthy
To Let in *The Forsyte Saga* (1922)

354. There, beside her in a lawn-coloured frock with narrow black edges, he had watched the game, and felt the old thrill stir within him.
Ib.

355. It is a curious fact that, whenever there is a test match at Lord's, many prominent business men in the city become strangely unwell after luncheon.
Anonymous
Sheep at Lord's in Early Days

356. In the City they do not impress one as having the breadth and culture and dignity of Meredith's men, egoists though they were. They cannot rise superior to the background of office and Stock Exchange growing year by year cheaper and shoddier. But Lord's, on the day of the Eton and Harrow match, touches their souls with a magic of its own and they wear their traditions with grace and confidence.
Dudley Carew
England Over (1927)

357. Lord's cricket, cricket straight out of Debrett.
Sir Neville Cardus
The Summer Game (1929)

358. The name is magic. It is also magnificently Debrett. It has an aura loftily unique, a caché unmatched. It conjures to the mind not merely the aristocratic among the world's cricket fields but a social rallying point. Indeed there are many human beings, a trifle vague as to its origin and functions, who believe that it is firmly associated with our peerage rather than plain Mr. Lord.

John Marshall
Lord's (1969)

359. For your good cricketer the ends of the earth have come to a resting-point at Lord's, and wherever he may be at the fall of a summer's day his face should turn religiously towards Lord's.

Sir Neville Cardus
Days in the Sun (1924)

360. It is said that the hardest-headed Australian has a quasi-religious respect for Lord's, and feels an extra urge to succeed there.

John Arlott
An Eye for Cricket (1979)

361. Lord's! What tender recollections
Does the famous name suggest!

Harry Graham
Lord's in Adam's Apples (1930)

362. I can never walk about Lord's without some such reflections as may be supposed in Rip Van Winkle after his sleep of twenty years: the present and the past come in such vivid contrast before my mind.

James Pycroft
Oxford Memories (1886)

363. The severance of Lord's from its almost immemorial rights and uses, would cause many a bitter pang and deep regret.

William Denison
Sketches of the Players (1846)

364. One fact seems sure;
That, while the Church approves, Lord's will endure.

Siegfried Sassoon
The Blues at Lord's in Satirical Poems (1926)

365. Few cricketers ever receive the accolade of a standing ovation at
Lord's, when, as the batsman approaches the pavilion, by a strange
unanimity of recognition, and with no suggestion of pre-
arrangement, the whole company of the members rise to their feet
with a rustling noise like the passing of a great flock of birds, and
the clapping gradually mounts to a crescendo.

John Arlott
An Eye for Cricket (1979)

366. Middlesex, to be frank, had not been a side worth going very many
miles to see, which of course was more than just a local misfortune,
for Lord's is the Mecca of all cricketers and a pilgrimage thereto
when they are in London provides a hallowed memory that must
sustain the faithful in many a barren outpost.

E. W. Swanton
Denis Compton: A Cricket Sketch (1948)

367. Lord's is the Valhalla of cricketers; countless days, famous for great
deeds, have come to a resting place at Lord's.

Sir Neville Cardus
The Summer Game (1929)

368. Marylebone is the *Omphalos*, the *Delos* of cricket.

Andrew Lang
The Badminton Library – Cricket (1904)

369. Cricket, lovely cricket,
At Lord's where I saw it;
Cricket, lovely cricket,
At Lord's where I saw it;
Yardley tried his best
But Goddard won the test.
They gave the crowd plenty fun;
Second Test and West Indies won.
With those two little pals of mine
Ramadhin and Valentine.

Lord Beginner
1950 Victory Calypso

370. Iredale says that he can never see a ball at Lord's when he is facing
the pavilion, and English cricketers have told me the same thing.

Walter A. Bettesworth
Chats on the Cricket Field (1910)

71. When Lord, who held the lease of the present Lord's ground, seemed to be 'topping the officer' over the M.C.C., and there were fears of its falling into the builders' hands, Mr. Ward asked him what he would take for it, and Lord named the extravagant sum of 5,000 l. 'Give me a pen and I will,' replied Mr. Ward and he wrote the cheque.

Frederic Gale
The Game of Cricket (1887)

72. The Oval, Canterbury, Brighton, and Fenner's always produced good wickets; but Lord's was terribly bad, and it was said that the only respect in which its pitch resembled a billiard table was the pockets!

H. S. Altham
A History of Cricket – Volume One (1926)

73. On the fiery wickets then prevalent, especially at Lord's, he was altogether intimidating, and not a few of the best batsmen of the time were known to retire precipitately towards square-leg.

(of John Jackson, Notts)
Ib.

74. But for a square patch of grass opposite the pavilion, which was kept constantly rolled, the ground was an affair of ridges and furrows, not improved by the number of old pitches which abounded. In those days anyone could have a pitch for a shilling, a sum which included the use of stumps, bat and ball.

Anonymous
Sheep at Lord's in Early Days

75. No human institution is perfect, but it would, in my opinion, be impossible to find nicer men than those who constitute the government of Lord's.

Sir Pelham Warner
Lord's 1787–1945 (1946)

76. From its inception, the Marylebone Club has been known for its sportsmanlike spirit, and to this day there is no ground whereon the game is more strictly played, none where the sporting element is more predominant, none whose habitués are more truly lovers of the game, or more free from partisan spirit.

A. E. Knight
The Complete Cricketer (1906)

377. The legs at Mary-le-bone never produced the least change in him; but, on the contrary, he was thoroughly disgusted at some of the manoeuvres that took place there from time to time.

John Nyren (of John Small in *The Cricketers of My Time*)
The Young Cricketer's Tutor (1833)

378. My own personal feeling is that the laws and regulations of cricket generally could not have been entrusted to better hands than those of the M.C.C. The club has always set a high standard to the cricket world, and has never refused to consider reasonable suggestions from responsible cricketers. It has acted with the impartiality of the High Court of Appeal, and has always safeguarded the best interests of the game, without unduly interfering with the rights and liberties of cricketers, individually or collectively.

W. G. Grace
W.G. – Cricketing Reminiscences and Personal Recollections (1899)

Bats, Balls and Accessories

The British 'Sphere of Influence' – the cricket ball.

379. Differences in appearance between the casual player and what might be termed the practising cricketer are not, in fact, illusory. The casual tends to equip himself by chance purchase, made under necessity.

J. M. Kilburn
Overthrows (1975)

380. Who would think that a little bit of leather, and two pieces of wood, had such a delightful and delighting power!

Mary Russell Mitford
Our Village (1824–32)

381. Strange fascination of a wooden bat!
Weird magic hidden in a leathern ball!

D. L. A. Jephson
A Few Overs (1913)

382. A Bat, a Ball, two Wickets and a Field –
What *words* are these that can such magic yield!

George Francis Wilson
A Century of Fours – LIII in *Cricket Poems* (1905)

383. We use a rose-bush for a wicket,
But at least it makes for brighter cricket!

A. A. Thomson
Almost Cricket in *Out of Town* (1935)

384. Give me a willow wand and I
With hide and cork and twine,
From century to century
Will gambol round my shrine!

Rudyard Kipling
Cricket Humour

385. The most remarkable instance of a hybrid animal is the cricket-bat.

Mr Punch's Book of Sports
edited by J. A. Hammerton (1906)

386. You may have paid your Income Tax
And bought the wife a hat;
Adjusted each domestic bill;
Reduced anxiety to nil.
Quite likely, too, you've made your will;
But – *have you oiled your bat?*

F. A. J. Godfrey
The Vital Question in *The Bradfield Chronicle*

387. . . . green ledgers with red backs, like strong cricket balls beaten
flat.

Charles Dickens
Martin Chuzzlewit (1844)

388. The British 'Sphere of Influence' – the cricket ball.

Mr Punch's Book of Sports
edited by J. A. Hammerton (1906)

389. The allure of a cricket ball flying through space is too simple for words, inexplicable but equally irrefutable, making the great gulf between the level-tempered pleasure of the expert and the involuntary and unrestrained joy of the mere human being.

Hon. T. C. F. Prittie
Mainly Middlesex (1947)

390. 'Ay, there's a deal o' human natur' in a treble-seam, sir; it don't like getting knocked about any more than we do.'

E. W. Hornung
A Bowler's Innings in *Old Offenders and a Few Scores* (1923)

391. A cricket ball is a shining miracle of leather, cork and twine, but when dispatched by a bat swung by a Bonner or a Dexter it becomes a missile of enormous power and speed.

Gerald Brodribb
Hit for Six (1960)

392. When old familiar sounds I know
Float up – the heavy roller's sound
Clanking across the county ground –
The busy whirr no spring forgets
Of cricket balls in cricket nets.

Herbert Farjeon
The Call of May – W. G. Loquitor in *Cricket Bag* (1946)

393. Few people realise what a difference a new ball makes to the batsman; it goes cleaner and firmer off the bat than the old one, and, what is better than all, a hard new ball is much more difficult to twist than one that has had a hundred runs made off it.

A. G. Steel
The Badminton Library – Cricket (1904)

394. When leg-pads were first introduced they were worn *under* the trousers, as though the hardy cricketer was ashamed of his cowardice in wearing them.

Sir Spencer Ponsonby-Fane
Preface to *Lord's and the M.C.C.* (1914)

395. When Lord Frederic Beauclerk first saw leggings he never imagined they would be allowed in a match – 'so unfair to the bowler.'

James Pycroft
Oxford Memories (1886)

396. We should then see the cricketer come into the field, as of old, encased like an armadillo; much of the lightness and elegance now required would be exchanged for a carefulness about broken fingers and body bruises; and the interests of cricket would thus suffer by its introduction.

Cricketer (Letter to *Sporting Magazine*, 16 February 1828)
quoted by William Denison in *Sketches of the Players* (1846)

397. Boys are in the habit of putting on belts. This is a mistake, since the noise the belt makes may at times be mistaken for a catch at the wicket.

K. S. Ranjitsinhji
The Jubilee Book of Cricket (1897)

398. It is not possible to play a clean game dirtily clad.

E. H. D. Sewell
Well Hit! Sir (1947)

399. My only sweetheart is a bag –
A faithful girl of dark brown leather,
Who's travelled many a mile with me
In half a hundred sorts of weather.
Once more to clasp your friendly hand,
To tramp along, by Hope attended,
Dreaming of glances, drives and cuts
My dear old girl, how truly splendid!

Norman Gale
The Forerunners

400. Provide yourself with a box large enough to contain two bats, two or three balls, stumps, and a complete change of dress. It should have a small till-box, to hold your watch and jewellery.

Nicholas Wanostrocht
Felix on the Bat (1845)

Trials and
Tribulations

S. M. J. Woods
(1867–1931).

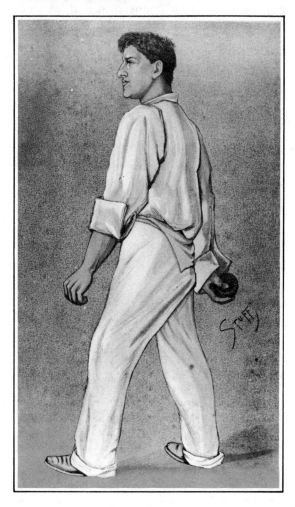

401. The players had to field in muffs and greatcoats, and such was the
cold they could scarcely feel the handle of the bat, or know whether
they had fielded the ball or not; indeed, such cricketing weather,
had never before been experienced.

Fred Lillywhite
The English Cricketers' Trip to Canada and the United States in 1859
(1860)

402. Let any man of common judgment see the velocity with which the ball flies from the bats of first-rate players, and how near the fieldsmen stand to the hitter; and then let him feel and weigh the ball in his hand, and he would naturally expect to hear that every public cricket ground was near connection with some casualty hospital, so deceptive is a prior reasoning.

James Pycroft
The Cricket Field (1851)

403. Cricket is not unattended with danger, resulting from inattention or inexperience; the accidents most commonly attendant upon players at cricket arising from unwatchfulness, or slowness of eye.

Charles Cowden Clarke
Introduction to John Nyren's <i>The Young Cricketer's Tutor</i> (1833)</div>

404. Moon: . . . Sometimes I dream of revolution, a bloody *coup d'etat* by the second rank – troupes of actors slaughtered by their understudies, magicians sawn in half by indefatigably smiling glamour girls, cricket teams wiped out by marauding bands of twelfth men.

Tom Stoppard
The Real Inspector Hound (1968)

405. Reiteration: Keep your promise – keep your temper – keep your wicket up.

William Davey
The Canterbury Cricket Week, 1865

406. Irritation: – ('Aye! there's the rub!' – Old Play) – I.Z. Bowlers are requested not to become rubbers of heads, hats, caps &c. – when a ball accidentally passes near a wicket. I.Z. Batsmen and Fieldsmen being hit at double or single wicket are not entitled to rub.

Ib.

407. I was playing too, and I vouch to you that it is true that in the first over a ball from Ernest Jones did go through W.G.'s beard, and that W.G. did rumble out a falsetto, 'What – what – what!' and that Harry Trott did say, 'Steady, Jonah' and that Ernest Jones did say, 'Sorry, doctor, she slipped.' Body-line bowling! W.G. topped the twenties, and his huge chest was black and blue.

C. B. Fry
Life Worth Living (1939)

408. I have seen his knuckles handsomely knocked about from Harris's bowling; but never saw any blood upon his hands – you might just as well attempt to phlebotomise a mummy.

John Nyren (of Tom Walker)
The Young Cricketer's Tutor (1833)

409. Yorkshire were in trouble, Tunnicliffe split a finger and J. T. Brown put his shoulder out bowling. I took off my boot and tried to put it (the shoulder) in at once, but couldn't manage it, although I had some one to sit on his head and others to hold him down. He was very sweaty from bowling, I couldn't get a firm grip on his arm, so he had to go to hospital to have it done. I am certain to this day that had he kept still it would have saved a lot of trouble. Poor fellow, I don't think he ever bowled again.

S. M. J. Woods
My Reminiscences (1925)

410. The ball hit him in the mouth, driving his lips through his teeth, and in writing him a letter of sympathy I could not help adding that I should advise him in future not to put his head where his bat ought to be.

Lord Harris
A Few Short Runs (1921)

411. Sometimes an unlucky boy will drive his cricket-ball full in my face.

Samuel Johnson
The Rambler – Number 30 (1750)

412. The worst accidents I have known have been from collision. Mr Slade, an eminent dentist, had to take the benefit of his own art to replace teeth knocked out while running with another to catch at ball at Lord's.

James Pycroft
Oxford Memories – Volume Two (1886)

413. Indeed so serious and so severe was the injury, that Mr Mynn was obliged to be packed up, as it were, and laid upon the roof of the stage coach, and in that position he rode from Leicester to London.

William Denison
Sketches of the Players (1846)

414. He played his cricket on the heath,
The pitch was full of bumps:
A fast ball hit him in the teeth,
The dentist drew the stumps.

Anonymous
Stumps Drawn!

415. Altogether it was an unfortunate game for his lordship, for during it
he had occasion to reprove one of the professionals, Stearman, for
slackness in the field. The latter lost his temper, and when the
chance came returned the ball so violently that it dislocated a finger,
which, neglected, came near to setting up lockjaw and cutting short
by ten years more of play that wonderful career.

H. S. Altham
A History of Cricket – Volume One (1926)

416. And if you thrive before you die
Till a hundred years be past,
They'll say he 'scored a centurie,
And his bails are off at last.'

Frederic Gale
An Old Cricket Hymn

417. As in life so in death lies a bat of renown,
Slain by a lorry (three ton);
His innings is over, his bat is laid down:
To the end a poor judge of a run.

George McWilliam
Epitaph

418. The danger of being hurt by the fastest of travelling balls is
infinitesimal, if we can but see the ball; and when unable to do so,
it is quite time to retire or to start cricket-writing and theorising.

A. E. Knight
The Complete Cricketer (1906)

419. A careful analysis of this rather hysterical publicity which surrounds
Test matches leads one to the conclusion that far too many people
are permitted to write about them.

J. C. Clay
Glamorgan County Cricket Club Year Book (1937)

Reflections

*Memories of matches
lost and won,
Of summer afternoons
and sun.*

420. Every age of cricket has its contemporary detractors.

Hon. T. C. F. Prittie
Mainly Middlesex (1947)

421. The cricket of the day has never throughout history been regarded
as wholly satisfactory. It becomes so only in retrospect: nor has the
game ever been conducted in an air of holy calm. As a red-blooded
exercise it has sometimes aroused hot passions, as a living art its
evolution has needed to be steered and channelled, from time to
time, by legislation.

E. W. Swanton
A History of Cricket – Volume Two (1962)

422. Cricket does not seem to produce the personalities nowadays.

H. M. Herman
How's That? (1937)

423. Memories of matches lost and won,
Of summer afternoons and sun,
Of many a doughty innings played,
Of catches missed and catches made.

Alfred Cochrane
The Master's Match, 1889–1914 in *Later Verses* (1918)

424. Imperial Summer bows her golden head –
The wickets are laid low, the Bails are shed.

George Francis Wilson
Summer's Ending in *Cricket Poems* (1905)

425.   the curving flight
Of sixes; the perennial delight
Of stolen runs; the lovely panther-leap
Of one fantastic catch.
All these are ours, to keep
And talk of on some bleak December night.

Dorothy Spring
Last Match

426. Now in Maytime to the wicket
Out I march with bat and pad:
See the son of grief at cricket
Trying to be glad.

A. E. Housman
A Shropshire Lad (1896)

427. Even as we pitch our wicket, flickering near
Are shades of men who found this cricket dear
And sealed their happy ventures ere we came.

Thomas Moult
Prelude to Cricket in *Some Cover Shots* (1924)

428. Recorded centuries leave no trace
On memory of that timeless grace.

John Arlott
On a Great Batsman

9. When Time of all our flannelled hosts
Leaves only the renown,
Our cracks, perhaps, may join the ghosts
That roam on Windmill Down,
Where shadowy crowds will watch the strife,
And cheer the deeds of wonder
Achieved by giants whom in life
A century kept asunder.

Alfred Cochrane
England Past and Present in *Collected Verses* (1903)

0. Lords and Commons Cricket is older than the County
Championship and older than almost all the first-class county clubs.

Eric E. Bullus
A History of Lords and Commons Cricket (1959)

1. There's music in the names I used to know,
And magic when I heard them, long ago.
'Is Tyldesley batting?' Ah, the wonder still!
. . . The school clock crawled, but cricket thoughts would fill
The last slow lesson-hour deliciously.

Thomas Moult
Names in *Some Cover Shots* (1924)

2. But for an hour to watch them play,
Those heroes dead and gone,
And pit our batsmen of today
With those of Hambledon!
Our Graces, Nyrens, Studds, and Wards
In weeks of sunny weather,
Somewhere upon Elysian swards,
To see them matches together!

Alfred Cochrane
England, Past and Present in *Collected Verses* (1903)

433. It is little I repair to the matches of the Southron folk,
Though my own red roses there may blow;
It is little I repair to the matches of the Southron folk,
Though the red roses crest the caps, I know.
For the field is full of shades as I near the shadowy coast,
And a ghostly batsman plays to the bowling of a ghost,
And I look through my tears on a soundless-clapping host
　　As the run-stealers flicker to and fro,
　　　To and fro;
　　O my Hornby and my Barlow long ago!
Francis Thompson
At Lord's in The Collected Poetry (1913)

434. Genius, however, is a personal force, bringing rather than acquiring
knowledge. Its scope is widened by enlarged opportunity, but not
essentially altered in character thereby. Hence it seems perfectly
natural to praise the greatness of the past player without any hint of
his superiority or inferiority to present-day greatness.
A. E. Knight
The Complete Cricketer (1906)

435. I think we must have been more intense in those days. Perhaps it is
that we were younger.
A. G. Gardiner
Pillars of Society (1913)

436. I can't bear to see anything like cowardice in cricket. Before the
days of pads and gloves and billiard-table grounds the game was
much harder, and only the good men came to the fore.
Frederic Gale
The Life of the Hon. Robert Grimston (1885)

437. Really, when you come to think of it, bowling is the most
important thing in the game. It's the brainiest part of cricket.
H. M. Herman
How's That? (1937)

438. Throughout its lengthening history cricket, whether you regard it as a sport, a way of life or an art form, has been graced by a number of individuals whose 'noticeable superior quality' in one or more of the basic skills has placed them apart from and above their more humdrum contemporaries.

John Parker
Cricket Styles and Stylists (1979)

439. Before 1914 it was beauty that counted in cricket – elegance of strokes, stylishness of bowling action, quixotry in captaincy. The gallant gesture was just as important as the mammoth score, the picturesque as the efficient.

W. J. Edrich
Cricket Heritage (1948)

440. Whereas Cricket is often called a trinity of games, of which one member is fielding, fielding itself, though regarded as a single occupation, involves a multitude of arts and too often a multitude of sins.

E. F. Benson and Eustace H. Miles
The Cricket of Abel, Hirst and Shrewsbury (1903)

441. In point of style the old players did not play the steady game with maiden overs as at present. The defensive was comparatively unknown: both the bat and the wicket, and the style of bowling too, were all adapted to a short life and a merry one.

James Pycroft
The Cricket Field (1851)

442. I gritted my teeth, told myself not to be nervous, that I'd got to stay in whatever happened. As I started coming out of the entrance past the members in the pavilion they all stood up and began to cheer. Taking their cue from the members in the pavilion, the whole of the vast crowd followed suit. The walk towards the wicket seemed an age. I'd never heard anything like that cheering before. The roars buffeted my head and made my eyes swim.

It was the cricket-lover's reply to the attacks which had been going on against me for the past week.

R. E. S. Wyatt
Three Straight Sticks (1951)

443. Most of all there is the playing of a much-loved game on grounds one has known since teenage days – some of them with happy memories of outstanding performances, of wins against the clock, of championships won and lost, of days in the sun and days when we have watched the rain beating down or a howling gale hustling across the field.

Ray Illingworth
Yorkshire and Back (1980)

444. My fortune in cricket was to play when the first-class game was free and fast-flowing and with a county as concerned to play attractive and sporting cricket as to win.

H. A. Pawson
Runs and Catches (1980)

445. Cricket dimensions will always defy the metric system, that Roman legacy to Europe.

Robin Marlar
The Story of Cricket (1979)

446. There is no talk, none so witty and brilliant, that is so good as cricket talk, when memory sharpens memory, and the dead live again – and the old happy days of burned-out June revive. We shall not see them again. We lament that lost lightness of heart, 'for no man under the sun lives twice, outliving his day', and the day of the cricketer is brief.

Andrew Lang
Introduction to Richard Daft's *Kings of Cricket* (1893)

447. I tend to believe that cricket is the greatest thing that God ever created on earth.

Harold Pinter
Pinter on Pinter in *The Observer*, 5 October, 1980

448. They *must* make their hay while their sun shines. Age will soon bowl them out; younger aspirants tread closely on their heels; and all they have to look forward to, when the eye has lost its keenness, the arm its muscle, and the system its nerve, is the precarious existence of an umpire.

'Quid'
Jerks in from Short Leg (1866)

449. I can speak from personal experience when I state that there are few things more sad than having to leave one's eleven because of the relentless force of Anno Domini.

Lord Hawke
Recollections and Reminiscences (1924)

450. Allowance, too, must be made for the deep, concealed, yet aching sadness of men doomed by age to be lookers on merely at the game, when everything in them but their bodies – *hinc illae lacrimae!* – longs to be playing themselves.

Hugh de Selincourt
On the Village Green in *The Times*, 25 May 1937 and *M.C.C.*,
1787–1937 (1937)

451. *My* heart is as sound ever, and beats regular and true time to the tune of old grateful thoughts for long friendships.

John Nyren
The Young Cricketer's Tutor (1833)

452. They vanish, these immortal players, and we suddenly realise with astonishment that years have passed since we heard a passing mention of some of them. At one point they seem as much a part of the permanent scheme of things as the sun which glows upon their familiar faces and attitudes and the grass which makes the background for their portrait; and then, bless us, it is time for even them to go.

Edmund Blunden
Cricket Country (1944)

453. When the cricket season was over I felt a deep sadness. It was like the end of harvest.

Alison Uttley
Carts and Candlesticks (1948)

454. Having attracted good material, cricket seems to enhance it, and is as good a form of democracy as exists in the world of sport.

I. A. R. Peebles
Spinner's Yarn (1977)

455. My sudden descent from cricket's pinnacle was an appalling shock, but I was always buoyed up by the thought that the shoulder would mend and that I would return. When it became clear that this would never be so I had achieved a philosophical attitude and was happy and grateful in more modest successes. But still in my dreams I am, to my surprise, summoned to play for England.

Ib.

456. To the great painter, the thought of his first work accepted by the Academy will be his most abiding memory; to the great archaeologist, the remembrance of that last spadeful of earth thrown aside and the first few stones of a long-buried city at last exposed to view; to the big-game hunter, the thought of the first tiger slain; and to the cricketer, the vivid recollection of his first century for his county, or perhaps the memory of a single isolated stroke, when the ball went off the bat to the boundary at such tremendous speed and with that indescribable feeling that only batsmen can know and appreciate – the sign of a perfectly timed stroke, with brain, eye, wrist, and bat working in complete unison.

D. J. Knight
Cricket (1925)

457. It is only twenty years ago; in eternity nothing; in swift mortal span, a little more than a sleep and a waking. But since then, many friends have gone, during the would-be peace and senseless inevitable war; gone, too, a few enemies, if such we are silly enough to call those around us who love a different way from ours. Besides, it was only a game, nor even of its kind a game that mattered much to any except a few cricketers and cricketer-watchers, a few unsmiling statisticians, a few reporters, who cursed cricket for missing their trains for them and damned first slip for standing too wide to catch that very late, that almost posthumous cut. Yes, yes: but it was *us*; with one wicket to fall and 217 runs to make; and we saw no reason, on earth, above it, or below, why we shouldn't make them.

R. C. Robertson-Glasgow
46 Not Out (1948)

458. It sounds more sensible and civilised to agree that these things are relative; that the Golden Age, if it happened at all, happened the day before yesterday – and that it is a human tendency to make heroes out of the fairly ordinary people of our boyhood, whether they happen to have been Prime Ministers, soldiers, cricketers or merely uncles. Now this, within reason, is fair enough, but, though possibly true as far as it goes, it does not go far enough to mean anything profound. It is, like most human and all English rules, subject to frequent exceptions, and I am free to maintain that the age which began a little before the turn of the century and ended with the outbreak of the first world war was a true golden age, not only for cricket, but for many other good things.

A. A. Thomson
Cricket: The Golden Ages (1961)

459. Truly great players would be great in any age, but in that age there were so many of them. It was the general standard that was so immensely high. It was a great age by any instrument of measurement. It had power; it had gusto and zest; it had elegance; it had a serenely patrician look.

Ib.

The Spirit of the Game

An English cricketing crowd is as fair and as generous as any assembly of mortals may be.

460. I see alive the spark whose glow
Oncoming years will fan to flame,
And recognise in embryo
The National Game.

C. E. Hughes
The Infant Cricket

461. If you have a right ambition you will desire to excell all boys of
your age at cricket.

Lord Chesterfield
Letters to His Son (1774)

462. Behind the pomp and majesty of our summer game there has
always been a basic uneasiness.

Allen Synge
Strangers' Gallery (1974)

463. This wonderful passion, this comradeship of feeling, is often seen in school elevens, rarely in county or international sides to the same exalted extent.

A. E. Knight
The Complete Cricketer (1906)

464. In boys' cricket matches the batting side is apt to wait in a row on a bench and in full panoply. Whether this habit comes from keenness or mistrust I have never quite known.

R. C. Robertson-Glasgow
Cricket Prints (1943)

465. Should every county ground be closed and never another shilling of gate-money leave our pockets, cricket would still be in England's lifeblood drawing its undismayable devotees from every section of the nation: the cricket that has such a hold on the young that they take their bats to bed with them, and on the old that they cannot see half a dozen urchins in the street, with only a lamp-post for stumps without pausing for a minute or two to watch; the cricket that stirs up such a turmoil of hopes and fears in our breasts that to consult the barometer can be almost an anguish.

E. V. Lucas
English Leaves (1933)

466. Drinking the best tea in the world on an empty cricket ground – that, I think, is the final pleasure left to man.

C. P. Snow
Death Under Sail (1932)

467. Cricket to us, like you, was more than play,
It was a worship in the summer sun.

Edmund Blunden
Pride of the Village

468. Nor sweeter music in the world is found
Than that upon an English Cricket ground.

B. Ratcliffe Ellis
Cricket Music

469. If the chief asset of the game is its 'glorious uncertainty', then winter cricket, when the wearing of skates is a *sine qua non*, must be the most perfect of all pastimes.

F. S. Ashley-Cooper
Cricket Highways and Byways (1927)

470. Now the joys of this game are chiefly these:
A blazing sun and a gentle breeze;
A close-cut field and a shady spot
To ruminate over the runs you've got;
A clear, clean eye and a steady hand,
A nerve of steel, and a cheerful band
Of fellow cricketers, one and all
Ready to welcome what'er befall.

A. E. Chadwick
The Joyous Game

471. Few things are more deeply rooted in the collective imagination of the English than the village cricket match. It stirs a romantic illusion about the rustic way of life, it suggests a tranquil and unchanging order in an age of bewildering flux, and it persuades a lot of townsfolk that that is where they would rather be.

Geoffrey Moorhouse
The Best-Loved Game (1979)

472. For cricket, of whatever kind, is still at its best in the country; and the agrarian country sides, though seldom the most efficient and never the richest, are usually the pleasantest to watch.

Sir J. C. Squire
Introduction to Cardus' *Cricket* (1930)

473. I doubt if there be any scene in the world more animating or delightful than a cricket-match: – I do not mean a set match at Lord's Ground for money, hard money, between a certain number of gentlemen and players, as they are called – people who make a trade of that noble sport, and degrade it into an affair of bettings, and hedgings, and cheatings, it may be, like boxing or horse-racing; nor do I mean a pretty *fête* in a gentleman's park, where one club of cricketing dandies encounter another such club, and where they show off in graceful costume to a gay marquee of admiring belles, who condescend so to purchase admiration, and while away a long summer morning in partaking cold collations, conversing occasionally, and seeming to understand the game – the whole being conducted according to ball-room etiquette, so as to be exceedingly elegant and exceedingly dull. No! the cricket that I mean is a real solid old-fashioned match between neighbouring parishes, where each attacks the other for honour and a supper, glory and half-a-crown a man.

Mary Russell Mitford
Our Village (1824–32)

474. The late *Miss Corelli* once rather sarcastically dismissed cricket as 'just a matter of a piece of wood hitting a piece of leather'. Cricketers laughed at the definition; but *Miss Corelli* might well have been forced to it by watching club cricket.

Sir Neville Cardus
Learning to Bat in *The Manchester Guardian* and *Some Cover Shots* (1924)

475. The rich diversity of clubs and players has always been an important aspect of cricket's attraction.

E. W. Swanton
Sort of a Cricket Person (1972)

476. English cricket may be compared to an imposing edifice. The spacious foundations are formed by village matches. On that is raised the charming ground-floor of club cricket. The more austere and less irresponsible superstructure of county encounters appears majestic but severe. The cupola consists of Test Matches and is so elevated as to excite ambitious aspirations, but also so bleakly exposed as to lose recreative consciousness.

Sir Home Gordon
Club Cricket in England in *The Times*, 25 May 1937 and *M.C.C. 1787–1937* (1937)

477. It is a game for gentle men;
Entirely wrong that man's spare rib
Should learn the mysteries of spin.

Vernon Scannell
Wicket Maiden

478. There are three kinds of cricket-match girls: the girl who knows all about the game, who scores her brother's runs and keeps his bowling analysis, and takes not her eyes from the wickets while any play is to be seen; the girl who is in a state of interested bewilderment; and the girl who watches the game with her back.

E. V. Lucas
Cricket-Match Girls in *Some Cover Shots* (1924)

479. Looking back it is amusing that a few diehards were aghast to learn that the ladies would be admitted into the pavilion but the younger element were frankly delighted, and it was acknowledged as a proper and sensible arrangement.

Tom Watson
Ibis Cricket, 1870–1949 (1950)

480. A lady of my acquaintance whom, with that misplaced kindness that sometimes steals over me, I had invited to watch a match of cricket, answered 'No, thanks; nothing ever happens at cricket; it is just all waiting.'

R. C. Robertson-Glasgow
Cricket Prints (1943)

481. The game itself might be compared to other more generous liquors: exhilarating and exciting is it, like champagne; beneficial, cordial, and fortifying to the system even as port; or it may be better likened for its infinite variety to that nectarious compound of all that is exquisite in beverage – the old fashioned punch, as graphically described by John Nyren in his 'Cricketer's Guide'.

Charles Box
The English Game of Cricket (1877)

482. The game, whether it is called first-class or otherwise, is CRICKET, and any measure can only be a half-measure which aims at differentiating between the classes of cricket.

K. S. Ranjitsinhji
The Jubilee Book of Cricket (1897)

483. Since cricket became brighter, a man of taste can only go to an empty ground, and regret the past. Or else watch a second-class county match, and regret the future.

C. P. Snow
Death Under Sail (1932)

484. High and low, rich and poor, greet one another practically on an equality, and sad will be the day for England if Socialism ever succeeds in putting class v. class and thus ending sports which have made England.

Lord Hawke
Recollections and Reminiscences (1924)

485. Cricket is an ancient pastime: it ripened sweetly, it has endured nobly.

Thomas Moult
Bat and Ball (1935)

486. Cricket in action is as honest today as the timber from which its bats are made.

Ib.

487. The side was what mattered to everyone and when you get that attitude cricket can be a very happy game.

Ray Illingworth
Yorkshire and Back (1980)

488. Cricket is a team game in which the individual, nevertheless, at intervals and in his turn, is called upon to assert and exploit his individuality, without ever forgetting his obligations to the team.

Lord Tennyson
Sticky Wickets (1950)

489. Indeed, the *camaraderie* and good-fellowship of the cricket field, the tendency to forget social or class distinction, and to ascend beyond diffracted rays to the primal light shed by the united love of the game, had already moved the moralist to protest.

A. E. Knight
The Complete Cricketer (1906)

490. The best joy in cricket is the genuine exultation in the excellence of others, in the reputation of the side.

Ib.

491. The amateur element, infusing a spirit necessarily different to that, in the long run, possessed by the most hard-working of professionals, should be encouraged, even to the extent of including amateurs who do not quite rise up to the high professional standard.

Ib.

492. The amateur, he who plays the game when he can for the love of it alone, is not only an essential constituent in a well-constituted eleven, he is the best exponent of all sport which is tinctured by the humanities, and which is not removed entirely to a region of purely scientific skill. The force which a body of paid men can give you is, in the long run, allowing for individual exceptions, the force of consolidated mass, not of high elevation.

Ib.

493. Together we impell'd the flying ball:
Together waited in our tutor's hall:
Together joined in cricket's manly toil.

Lord Byron
Cricket at Harrow in *Hours of Idleness* (1807)

494. Cricket is essentially a co-operative sport – it is confined to no class: it is *best* practised where it is most *fused*.

'Quid'
Jerks in from Short Leg (1866)

495. 'Ah! that's the beauty of cricket!' declared old John heartily, wiping his face all over with a large handkerchief, 'that's the glorious beauty of cricket. Every single man-jack of us helped, one way or another to win that game.'

Hugh de Selincourt
The Cricket Match (1924)

496. Oh, I am so glad you have begun to take an interest in cricket. It is simply a social necessity in England.

P. G. Wodehouse
Piccadilly Jim (1918)

497. Is there life after cricket? First go through cricket, to earn the right to this unknown passage. Your discovery may be socially incommunicable: an unplayable wicket.

Marvin Cohen
Stranger's Gallery (1974)

498. Cricket, we have shown, was originally classed among the games of the lower orders; so we find the yeomen infinitely more superior to the gentlemen even before cricket had become by any means so much of a profession as it is now.

James Pycroft
The Cricket Field (1851)

499. I cannot see how cricket, as a great institution for providing popular amusement, could, as things are now, exist without a class of people who devote themselves entirely to it.

K. S. Ranjitsinhji
The Jubilee Book of Cricket (1897)

500. 'Steady on, old chap, he did play for the Gentlemen!'
'I know – but only once.'

Frank Launder and Sidney Gilliat
The Lady Vanishes (1938)

501. The cricket world, surely, is as crazy and as inconsistent as the outside one.

J. H. Fingleton
Brightly Fades the Don (1949)

502. When, in 1962, the distinction between amateurs and professionals was abolished and all first-class players were called 'cricketers', cricket was in the van, ahead of nearly every other sport, in accepting the facts of social and economic life.

Diana Rait Kerr and I. A. R. Peebles
Lord's, 1946–70 (1971)

503. And so if a team isn't winning, and you don't expect it to turn up on top, why you've got to root for it. Then if you root hard enough, why, you turn up a victory when it wasn't looked for. And then if you root every day the people call you a rooter, and they think you're a jolly good fellow because you don't lose heart, you know, but just keep on rooting until you bring things on top.

Anonymous
Philadelphia News (1899)

504. The whole subject of barracking can be summed up this wise. It is harmful or harmless, depending upon the temperament of the man barracked, and when a player has won his way to Test ranks his temperament should be such that he does not care a fig about it.

J. H. Fingleton
Cricket Crisis (1946)

505. Cricket is an exacting game of skill which demands a long apprenticeship. It is perhaps on account of these initial difficulties that cricket has never enjoyed any significant success on the Continent.

Allen Synge
Strangers' Gallery (1974)

506. But what care I? It's the game that calls me –
Simply to be on the field of play;
How can it matter what fate befalls me,
With ten good fellows and one good day!

A. A. Milne
The First Game

507. It is good to bowl with action high
Or to smite the leather hard and far,
But it's better to wear the proper tie
And to keep your end up at the bar.

Donald Hughes
The Short Cut

508. And the reward of it all? Of that we may be certain: the joy of
health and strength harnessed to an art and to a venture, the friends
that it brings to us, even if on the field of play they are foes, and
when you take off your pads, whether for the day, for the season, or
after long years for good, the memory of troubles halved and joys
doubled, because both have been shared with them.

H. S. Altham
The Importance of Coaching in *The Gillette Book of Cricket and Football*
edited by Gordon Ross (1963)

509. You do well to love it, for it is more free from anything sordid,
anything dishonourable, than any game in the world. To play it
keenly, honourably, generously, self-sacrificingly, is a moral lesson
in itself, and the classroom is God's air and sunshine. Foster it, my
brothers, so that it may attract all who can find time to play it;
protect it from anything that would sully it, so that it may grow in
favour with all men.

Lord Harris
Letter to *The Times* 2 February 1931

510. Cricket and church were alike holy. The flight of the ball, the swift,
graceful movement of the men, the swing of the bat, were as full of
praise as were the hymns we sang.

Alison Uttley
Carts and Candlesticks (1948)

511. His lightest interest was cricket, but he did not take that lightly. His
chief holiday was to go to a cricket-match, which he did as if he
was going to church; and he watched critically, applauded
sparingly, and was darkly offended by any unorthodox play.

H. G. Wells
The History of Mr Polly (1910)

512. Cricket is an art. Like all art it has a technical foundation. To enjoy
it does not require technical knowledge, but analysis that is not
technically based is mere impressionism.

C. L. R. James
Beyond a Boundary (1963)

513. A time will come, a time will come,
When the people sit with a peaceful heart,
Watching the beautiful, beautiful game,
That is battle and service and sport and art.

Arnold Wall
A Time Will Come

14. Cricket is simply the most catholic and diffused, the most innocent,
kindly, and manly of popular pleasures, while it has been the
delight of statesmen and the relaxation of learning.

Andrew Lang
Introduction to Richard Daft's *Kings of Cricket* (1893)

515. Out with your flannels, gloves, and bats,
And play the finest game on earth!

Norman Gale
The Bigot

516. It is astounding that cricket should have taken root in the English
climate. It almost makes me believe that our summers have grown
worse over the past few centuries, though people who have studied
the evidence say it is not so.

Alan Gibson
A Mingled Yarn

517. I had devoted far too much of my life to this utterly irrational
game. I would chuck the whole thing and take to Strindberg for
amusement.

A. A. Thomson
Cricket My Happiness (1955)

518. No one can be satisfied with the game as it is at present, especially
in a dry season with true and hard grounds – with innings of three
hundred and more runs no match has much interest.

James Pycroft
Oxford Memories – Volume Two (1886)

519. Cricket has appeared to deteriorate because, reflecting the times, it has changed. Most men, being conservative, do not like change unless it benefits themselves. With cricket now reflecting the uniformity of the welfare state, not to mention the vulgarity of the consumer society, it is not surprising that some middle-aged or elderly spectators long for a return to the cricket of the 1930s or (as they imagine it to have been) of the Edwardian age when the amateur presumably enjoyed £600 a year and a room of his own.

Kenneth Gregory
In Celebration of Cricket (1978)

520. The modern game was gripped to the point of suffocation in an iron band imposed by the gospel of containment, shackling the players so that they could not break out of their prison even if they would.

Diana Rait Kerr and I. A. R. Peebles
Lord's 1946–70 (1971)

521. If your emotional conduct on the field follow the modern fashion; that is to say, bowlers and fielders may leap and wave their arms in the air when asking the umpire for a decision. The batsman on the whole maintains a dead-pan expression; but, if struck by a rising ball, he may show his pain or disapproval by throwing his bat and gloves on the ground, or even checking up on his dentures by taking them out and putting them back again.

R. C. Robertson-Glasgow
How to Become a Test Cricketer (1962)

522. But the gum-chewing habit is very catching; and you will sometimes see a whole fielding team resembling a herd of cows at pasture.

Ib.

523. Against the increased tempo of modern life cricket must be regarded as rather a slow-moving activity. Nevertheless I believe that cricket represents something traditional in the English way of life which will always command enough support to keep its head above water.

H. S. Altham
Evidence to Lords Tribunal, 1959, quoted in *Lord's 1946–1970* (1971)

524. Cricket's main charm is its slow, reflective tempo, its pauses for mental mastication and digestion and its lack of bustle and rush.

Hon. T. C. F. Prittie
Lancashire Hot-Pot (1949)

525. Cricket is the queerest game,
Every stroke is just the same –
Merely whacking at a ball;
Nothing else to see at all.
Then there comes some big surprise
When I chance to close my eyes.

Anonymous

526. I was brought up to believe that cricket is the most important activity in men's lives, the most important thread in the fabric of the cosmos.

Bernard Hollowood
Cricket on the Brain (1970)

527. Cricket is a very humanising game. It appeals to the emotions of local patriotism and pride. It is eminently unselfish; the love of it never leaves us, and binds all the brethren together, whatever their politics and rank may be.

Andrew Lang
Introduction to Richard Daft's *Kings of Cricket* (1893)

528. An English cricketing crowd is as fair and as generous as any assembly of mortals may be.

Ib.

529. But it is to be feared that the last word has not been written on the subject of uninformed barracking. Cricket must not, in the meantime, be allowed to become the cockshy of the bucks and bumpkins whose spiritual homes are the prize-ring and the greyhound track. The voices only of those who love the game must be heard.

Hon. T. C. F. Prittie
Lancashire Hot-Pot (1949)

530. The cream of cricket is being thrown away. Soon we will be left with only a gobbet of the synthetic equivalent – floating in skimmed milk.

Ib.

531. Cricket transcends the individual. It has a life of its own and in interaction with it the humblest of us may be raised to a kind of greatness, the most domineering be reduced to a nullity.

Ib.

532. There can be raw pain and bleeding where so many thousands see the inevitable ups and downs of only a game.

C. L. R. James
Beyond a Boundary (1963)

533. Cricket is first and foremost a dramatic spectacle. It belongs with the theatre, ballet, opera and the dance.

Ib.

534. There has always been a singularly close affinity between cricket and the stage, helped no doubt by the fact that actors are apt to have plenty of leisure during the day.

E. W. Swanton
Sort of a Cricket Person (1972)

535. Reading poetry and watching cricket were the sum of my world, and the two are not so far apart as many aesthetes might believe.

Philip Lindsay
Don Bradman (1951)

536. Because we play cricket and like it well, we need be no strangers at the banquet where the rich wine of high converse passes, nor need the great teachers of truths greet us as of foreign tongue. It is quite possible for us to play cricket with the thought that it be good.

A. E. Knight
The Complete Cricketer (1906)

537. Cricket makes for tolerance and kindly feelings, for wholesome self-denial and restraint; it smooths out the lines of hard features with the softening touch of joy in natural delight and cultivated skill; it enriches many a close, cabined life with hours of refreshment and relief, and cultivates many a sterile spot.

Ib.

538. Almost all the evils of excessive athleticism concern the class entirely devoted to its exploitation, in far less degree do they touch the hundreds of thousands of spectators whose hearts are delivered over to the enthusiasm of it, turned from their own close centre.

Ib.

539. As a matter of unfortunate fact, the great majority of our townsfolk have not reasonable opportunities to join in the great outdoor game; never have the opportunities to become familiarised with the great emergencies of the cricket-field; never have the sight trained and tested, the muscles hardened and developed, the nerves strengthened, the hearing proved, which is the cricket way of making honest and healthy Englishmen.

Ib.

540. There is value and discipline in duty, but only in those rare and happy moments when desire and duty run hand in hand is there shown the high possibilities of cricket.

Ib.

541. The noblest fires, whether of batting or bowling, can be fed only by the concurrent culture of every power we have.

Ib.

542. All sport, if it is to be as delight giving as it may be, must embody an element of creative art, of generation, not of technical skill alone.

Ib.

543. In the very breadth of its humanity, its sweet simplicities, its open-air fragrance and charm, the game of cricket appeals to nearly all men.

Ib.

544. The greatest of cricket skill is not born of conscious care: it breathes happy instincts which shrink with spontaneity from all that is inartistic and unfitting; but bowling and batting and fielding which are nobly aimed at, are bound to be more or less nobly expressed.

Ib.

545. We still like to get our fifties and hundreds apart from anything of a monetary character accruing, once certain, now problematical. There is a joy in craftsmanship which is very sweet, and the cold calculations of the market are after-thoughts to it.

Ib.

546. A game primarily, it is now so extended in its operations as to make business transactions necessary. The real problem is to infuse the chivalrous spirit of fair-mindedness for which sport stands into whatever business relations are not inevitable.

Ib.

547. The modern cricket world is given over to average mongering and money making.

Ib.

548. The cricket-field is far beyond the breaking-in business of a military camp: you cannot be drilled in it by any parade exercise, you will have to develop an individual skill.

Ib.

549. No one thing would make cricket more busy in the best sense than a desire to get, not the risky but every possible certain run – certain, that is, to keen players, not to exceptionally fast runners.

Ib.

550. It is a whole and wholesome game of cricket that we want, not a mere exciting climax.

Ib.

551. What matters is that the games, win or lose, should be good games, well worth playing and having been played, well worthy of remembrance.

Hugh de Selincourt
On the Village Green in *The Times*, 25 May 1937 and *M.C.C.*
1787–1937 (1937)

552. Cricket is no excuse for ignorance.

Barry Perowne
Raffles of the M.C.C. (1979)

553. For cricket affords to a race of professionals a merry and abundant, though rather a laborious livelihood, from the time that the May-fly is up to the time the first pheasant is down.

James Pycroft
The Cricket Field (1851)

554. The game of cricket, philosophically considered, is a standing panegyric on the English character: none but an orderly and sensible race of people would so amuse themselves.

Ib.

555. That cricket is partly a game of chance there can be no doubt; but that all is chance that men call such, we strenuously deny.

Ib.

556. Still is a cricket-field a sphere of wholesome discipline in obedience and good order; not to mention that manly spirit that faces danger without shrinking, and bears disappointment with good nature.

Ib.

557. There is something highly intellectual in our noble and national pastime. But the cricketer must possess certain qualifications, not only physical and intellectual, but moral qualifications also; for of what avail is the mind to design and the hand to execute, if a sulky temper paralyses his exertions and throws a damp upon the field; or if impatience dethrones judgment, and the man hits across good balls, because loose balls are long in coming; or again, if a contentious and imperious disposition leaves the cricketer all 'alone in his glory', voted the pest of every eleven.

Ib.

558. In one word, there is no game in which amiability and an unruffled temper is so essential to success, or in which virtue is rewarded half as much as in the game of cricket.

Ib.

559. Great is the power of comedy. Gradually ill-temper faded, and men remembered that they had come to watch an entertainment and not to take part in a squalling match.

Robert Lynd
Malice and Warwick Armstrong (1921) in *Some Cover Shots* (1924)

560. Nothing that the law-makers or the law-breakers or the M.C.C. or the Board of Control or any conferences or county committees or pressmen or captains or players can do to it or have done to it over the years – nothing can affect cricket's basic worth or irresistible attraction.

Ben Travers
The Infatuee in *The Cricketer's Bedside Book* (1966)

561. This is not to say that the old infatuee does not nurse his grievances. First and foremost, to his way of thinking, the administration of the game has, of recent years, been based on a cardinal fallacy, namely that the greatest attraction cricket has to offer is easy run getting under conditions favouring the same. This has not only resulted in the discouragement and gradual elimination of the spin bowler; it goes deeper than that. It means that the younger generation never, or very seldom, has the chance of seeing the most enthralling spectacle cricket has to offer, the absorbing, anguishing fascination of watching great batsmanship on a ruined wicket.

Ib.

562. Great fast bowling opposed to great batting must represent the most thrilling of personal encounters because of the manifest physical element, but the student observer can derive long-lasting satisfaction from skilled batting meeting the subtleties of slow bowling.

J. M. Kilburn
Overthrows (1975)

563. All good things done well are beautiful. There is much more in a fine off-drive or a well-bowled ball than the resulting fourer or wicket.

K. S. Ranjitsinhji
The Jubilee Book of Cricket (1897)

564. Cricket has got to have the courage of its own aristocracy.

Dudley Carew
To The Wicket (1946)

565. The ultimate prosperity of first-class cricket must be based on the merits of first-class cricket.

J. M. Kilburn
Overthrows (1975)

566. Cricket was a dance with a bat in your hand, or with the encumbrance of a ball. What was exquisite and memorable was the lyric movement of the artist in action. What was incidental was the score that resulted from his having a bat in his hands, or the analysis that came about from his handling of the ball.

Denzil Batchelor
C. B. Fry (1951)

567. It is, indeed, lamentably but irrefutably true that personality no longer plays its former part on the cricket field. But cricket has done no more than march with the times.

> Hon. T. C. F. Prittie
> *Mainly Middlesex* (1947)

568. Cricket, like the novel, is great when it presents men in the round, when it shows the salty quality of humanity.

> John Arlott
> *Cricket* (1953)

569. So great is the variety of fortune and so wide is the range of tests which the player must face in cricket that it is not surprising that we have borrowed so many cricket expressions to explain situations in everyday life. Cricket requires tenacity, determination, courage, patience, skill, stamina, unlimited concentration and, above all, sportsmanship. I cannot believe that there is any game which demands more of a player or which is of such absorbing interest to the spectator who has troubled to understand something of it. Cricket is and can be a life in itself. It is a game, but it is more than a game.

> R. E. S. Wyatt
> *Three Straight Sticks* (1951)

570. Cricket is certainly a very good and wholesome exercise, yet it may be abused if either great or little people make it their business.

> *Gentleman's Magazine* (1743)

571. 'Cricket,' he once remarked, 'was intended to be played between twenty-two sportsmen for their own pleasure; it was never meant to be the vehicle for international competition, huge crowds and headline news – otherwise it wouldn't have been given a code of laws with such gaps as you could drive through with a coach and horses.'

> B. H. Lyon
> quoted by John Arlott in *An Eye for Cricket* (1979)

572. Without doubt the laws of cricket and the conduct of the game are a great example to the world.

> Sir Donald Bradman
> *Farewell to Cricket* (1950)

573. A Kent player sat down to get wind after a run, his bat in his ground but with his seat of honour out, and for a moment let go the handle, and the wicket-keeper stumped him out! He was very angry and said he would never play again; however, he did play the return match at Canterbury, where he was put out in precisely the same manner.

James Pycroft
The Cricket Field (1851)

574. An unpleasant incident occurred during the second day. Kenny Postman reached a debut 50 with a single and Gary Gower, having safely made his own ground, walked up the pitch to congratulate the batsman, only for the Free State 'keeper to remove his bails and appeal successfully for run out.

Robert Brooke
Cricket in Isolation in *Pelham Cricket Year – Two* (1980)

575. The chief qualifications to be looked for when considering likely selectors, it would seem, are the thickest possible skin, a complete ignorance of all aspects of cricket, the facility for attracting bribes, a longing for power, and a closed and prejudiced mind.

Douglas Insole
The Boundary Book (1962)

576. All are affected and influenced by a wider world conditioned by the changing times, so that factors which in themselves have nothing to do with cricket, can affect their attitude to the game.

Leslie Duckworth
The Story of Warwickshire Cricket (1974)

577. Cricket is always vulnerable to private promoters or pirate captains motivated only by the need for more money from it.

Robin Marlar
The Story of Cricket (1979)

578. Heavenly weather really. If life was always like that. Cricket weather. Sit around under sunshades. Over after over. Out. They can't play it here. Duck for six wickets. Still Captain Buller broke a window in the Kildare Street Club with a slog to square leg.

James Joyce
Ulysses (1922)

579. They knew that cricketers should be ardent, alert.

Charles Morgan
Portrait in a Mirror (1929)

580. All of us bring an agony of concern to the job we do; few of us derive from it such an emotional and aesthetic sense of fulfilment as the professional cricketer.

David Lemmon
Summer of Success (1980)

581. We never forget that cricket is a game, that there are things more fundamental to the act of living and dying, but in a world where every day someone murders or is murdered in the name of some satanic cause, there is a refreshing breath of sanity in intellect and emotion spent in the honesty of physical endeavour.

Ib.

582. Was it not Groucho Marx, who, when watching his first match of cricket at Lord's, remarked to his companion and guide 'But say, when's the game *itself* going to begin?'

R. C. Robertson-Glasgow
How to Become a Test Cricketer (1962)

583. And brighter cricket, at all events, will result only from the initiative and intelligence of county captains on the field and county committees at the council table. The future of the game should be left in their safe keeping.

Hon. T. C. F. Prittie
Lancashire Hot-Pot (1949)

584. The spirit of cricket ordains that one should die fighting.

Ib.

585. Cricket, however, has more in it than mere efficiency. There is something called the spirit of cricket, which cannot be defined.

Lord Tennyson
Sticky Wickets (1950)

586. There's a breathless hush in the Close to-night –
Ten to make and the match to win –
A bumping pitch and a blinding light,
An hour to play and the last man in.
And it's not for the sake of a ribboned coat
Or the selfish hope of a season's fame,
But his captain's hand on his shoulder smote:
'Play up! play up! and play the game!'

> Sir Henry Newbolt
> *Vitai Lampada* in *Admirals All and Other Verses* (1897)

587. Cricket is the greatest outdoor game in the world. He who plays it
in the right spirit learns endurance, is taught to keep his temper
under trying circumstances, gives up his own selfish interests for the
sake of the general good, and practises himself in doing a hard day's
work, when eye and hand and foot are hard put to it, to overcome
rivals in healthy combat.

> Bishop Henry Montgomery
> *The History of Kennington and its Neighbourhood* (1889)

588. That it is not wholly unconnected with some of the high and
honour-stirring principles of Moral Philosophy, is a suggestion
which may hazard the contempt of the self-sufficient; nevertheless,
we are prepared with good evidence in favour of our statement.

> Nicholas Wanostrocht
> *Felix on the Bat* (1845)

589. The whole edifice of Christian virtues could be raised on a basis of
good cricket.

> Edward Cracroft Lefroy
> Letter quoted in W. A. Gill's *Edward Cracroft Lefroy: His Life and
> Poems* (1897)

590. Cricket began when first a man-monkey, instead of catching a
cocoa-nut thrown him playfully by a fellow-anthropoid, hit it away
from him with a stick which he chanced to be holding in his hand.

> H. G. Hutchinson
> *Cricket* (1903)

591. To some people cricket is a circus show upon which they may or
may not find it worth while to spend sixpence; to others it is a
pleasant means of livelihood; to others a physical fine art full of
plot, interest and enlivened by difficulties; to others in some sort it
is a cult and a philosophy, and these last will never be understood
by the profanus vulgus, nor by the merchant-minded nor by the
unphysically intellectual.

C. B. Fry
Foreword to D. L. A. Jephson's A Few Overs (1913)

592. O wonderful game that does so much towards the formation of
character, that inculcates discipline, self-control, and even-handed
conduct.

W. R. Weir
The Public School Spirit in Some Cover Shots (1924)

593. No game except cricket combines a great amount of science with
the advantage of bodily exercise. In fact, the mental and physical
qualities required for one who would excel as a cricketer are about
equally in demand.

Richard Daft
Kings of Cricket (1893)

594. It would be a pretty world, if we all had something to do, just to
make the leisure the pleasanter, and green merry England were
sprinkled all over 'of afternoons' with gallant fellows in white
sleeves, who threshed the earth and air of their cricket-grounds into
a crop of health and spirits; after which they should read, laugh,
love and be honourable and happy beings, bringing God's work to
its perfection, and suiting the divine creation they live in . . .
Nature is stirring and so is the cricketer. Nature, in a hundred
thousand parts to a fraction, is made up of air, and fields and
country and out-of-doors, and a strong teeming earth, and a good-
natured sky; and so is the strong heart of the cricketer.

Leigh Hunt
Cricket and Exercise in General in The Seer; or, Common-places
Refreshed (1840–41)

595. I can think of many energetic and successful business men who
would be contributing much more to the public service were they
playing county cricket well for six days in the week.

Sir J. C. Squire
Introduction to Cardus' Cricket (1930)

596. In spite of recent jazzed-up matches, cricket to be fully appreciated demands leisure, some sunny warm days, and an understanding of its finer points – and as it depends more than any other ball game on varying conditions, on the state of the pitch, on weather and wind and light, it multiplies its fine points. Though it is often considered a 'gentlemanly game', an idea supported by its leisurely progress and breaks for lunch, tea, cool drinks on the field, we must remember that many of its greatest performers came from the Industrial North, which also supplied, until our own time, large numbers of its most knowledgeable and keenest spectators.

J. B. Priestley
The English (1973)

597. Will Rogers, I am afraid, had the answer when, on his only visit to a cricket match, he was asked by the then Prince of Wales for any suggested improvements in the game. He pulled at his forelock and said: 'Well, your Highness, if I was in charge I'd line up all the players before the game and say, 'Now listen, fellers, no food till you're through.'

Alastair Cooke
Manchester Guardian (1954) and *In Celebration of Cricket* (1978)

598. Cricket never was and never can be a game of continuous excitement or of great achievement every day. The quiet hours, the simple strivings, are as much a part of the attraction as the unforgettable moments of high drama. Cricket is a composite joy, a blending of the modest and the magical.

J. M. Kilburn
Cricket Decade (1959)

599. For a game of cricket is at work from the first ball to the last in shaping an outline and design for itself; sometimes the design degenerates into dullness and incompetence and a man may waste his time in looking for subtlety in the motive that prompts a batsman to pat a half-volley carefully to mid-off, but design there always is and there is interest even in the tracing of the course and impulse of its failure.

Dudley Carew
To the Wicket (1946)

00. In every game there is a moment of destiny, a moment when fortune hesitates which way she will incline, when the genius of the match is poised and is ready to follow the side which has the courage and intelligence to take charge of her.

Ib.

01. But cricket is full of glorious chances, and the goddess who presides over it loves to bring down the most skilful players.

Thomas Hughes
Tom Brown's School Days (1857)

02. Cricket as a passion is distinctly contagious.

David Frith
England versus Australia (1981)

03. And from here and there came the sounds of the cricket bats through the soft grey air. They said: pick, pack, pock, puck: little drops of water in a fountain slowly falling in the brimming bowl.

James Joyce
Portrait of the Artist as a Young Man (1916)

04. He does not know how to handle a bat
Any more than a dog or a cat.

William Blake
An Island in the Moon (1787)

05. I am sure that the Almighty never intended that cricket should be played in anything but golden sunshine, especially if the wicket was doing a bit.

Ray Illingworth
Yorkshire and Back (1980)

06. Give me a day in drenching May,
Give me a ball to bowl,
Give me a pitch, I'll count me rich,
And you can have the whole
Terrestrial earth for what it's worth,
Including the North Pole!

Herbert Farjeon
Bitter Sweet in *Cricket Bag* (1946)

607. Temple and I talked of the ancient raptures of a first of May cricketing-day on a sunny green meadow, with an ocean of a day before us, and well-braced spirits for the match.

George Meredith
The Adventures of Harry Richmond (1871)

608. There is only one drawback to the first match of the season – sweet as are the odours of the fresh spring flowers, invigorating as is the incense offered to the metropolitan nostril by nature in her new clothing of the early summer, delicious as is the first night's rest after the first match of the season, inevitable and indescribable is the stiffness that warps the muscles next morning, when the joints rattle like internal crackers; and sit as you will during that day and the next, on the easiest ottoman and downyest sofa, you will be reminded at every stir of your first day's cricket in the country.

'Quid'
Jerks in from Short Leg (1866)

609. Self-confidence at cricket, like at any other pursuit, is invaluable, but it is very rarely to be imparted; it may be acquired by long practice.

Ib.

610. We are loth to admit, but we are very much afraid it is a growing evil, that professional cricket is lapsing into £ s. d.

Ib.

611. Amongst cricketers, the pleasure is heightened by the conviction that their pastime is untainted by vulgarity and cruelty; and that their fair countrywomen may witness of prowess of a brother, a lover, or a husband, without a blush, or the painful sense of impropriety.

Frederick Lillywhite
On Cricket in *The Young Cricketer's Guide* (third edition) (1850)

612. But there is something in the game of cricket which cannot be expressed in words – a peculiar charm and fascination. It is as impossible to describe this as it is to describe the pleasure derived from seeing fine trees or fine buildings.

K. S. Ranjitsinhji
The Jubilee Book of Cricket (1897)

13. It is a mistake to suppose that whatever is not forbidden in written laws may be done without self-condemnation. Nor does it follow that what is felt to be contrary to the advantage of cricket ought to be made a matter of legislation.

Ib.

14. No human institution is perfect: it will always tend to excess or defect.

Ib.

15. Hail Cricket! glorious, manly, British game!
First of all Sports! be first alike in fame!

James Love
Cricket: An Heroic Poem (1744)

16. Willow the King is a monarch grand;
Three in a row his courtiers stand;
Every day, when the sun shines bright,
The doors of his palace are painted white,
And all the company bow their backs
To the King with his collar of cobbler's wax.

E. E. Bowen
Harrow Songs and Other Verses (1886)

17. Flush'd with his rays, beneath the noontide sun,
In rival bands, between the wickets run,
Drive o'er the sward the ball with active force,
Or chase with nimble feet its rapid course.

Lord Byron
Cricket at Harrow in *Hours of Idleness* (1807)

18. While roses blow the cricket-field is yours.
Measure their season: so your lease endures.
Match with their fragrance every fruitful sound:
Tread worthily this sunlit slip of ground.

Thomas Moult
While Roses Blow

19. Patient, dramatic, serious, genial,
From over to over the game goes on,
Weaving a pattern of hardy perennial,
Civilisation under the sun.

Gerald Bullett
Village Cricket in *News from the Village* (1952)

620. It was a great game, and exciting and dramatic and even at times tragic – but funny it emphatically was not.

Sir J. C. Masterman
Fate Cannot Harm Me (1935)

621. Above all, do not get sent to the boundary position, unless you are a natural comedian and are prepared to make the crowd laugh.

R. C. Robertson-Glasgow
How to Become a Test Cricketer (1962)

622. The central theme was to hit the ball hard and enjoy it, and play beautiful cricket. It was a humbling experience that the nearer I came to achieving my aim the more I was aware of my inadequacies and imperfections.

T. C. Dodds
Hit Hard and Enjoy It (1976)

623. Last Munday youre Father was at Mr. Payns and plaid at Cricket and come home pleased anuf, for he struck the best Ball in the game and whishd he had not anything else to do he wuld play at Cricket all his Life.

Mary Turner, of East Hoathly, Sussex
Letter to her son at Brighthelmstone (1739)

624. Cricket is an altogether too sacred thing to him to be tampered with on merely religious grounds.

H. G. Wells
Certain Personal Matters (1898)

625. Casting a ball at three straight sticks and defending the same with a fourth.

Rudyard Kipling

The Player

526. Then ye returned to your trinkets; then ye
      contented your souls
With the flannelled fools at the wicket or
      the muddied oafs at the goals.

                      Rudyard Kipling
                      The Islanders

527. He knew plenty about fighting, and afterwards of horse-racing; but a man cannot learn the odds of cricket unless he is something of a player.

                      James Pycroft
                  The Cricket Field (1851)

528. Who ever hoped like a cricketer?

                      R. C. Robertson-Glasgow
                  Cricket Prints (1943)

629. The cricket player is not an actor on a stage, merely a personality to be lost in the creation of a poet's brain or a playwright's mind; he is himself the poet and the playwright.

A. E. Knight
The Complete Cricketer (1906)

630. The spirit which inclines us to regard as a mercenary the player who leaves for higher emolument is the true spirit of a game, and tends in its reverse aspect to keep the eye wide open for our own fresh youth, to the resolve to nurture our own plot with an intense and deliberate culture.

Ib.

631. Cricketers, being human, are not over-ready to do what is irksome or distasteful, even where they recognise that it is for their own good and that of others.

K. S. Ranjitsinhji
The Jubilee Book of Cricket (1897)

632. A cricketer is just a man with a clear eye, bronzed face, and athletic figure. He is usually somewhat lacking in general information, and is sometimes a poor conversationalist upon any but his own subject. He does not read much. On the other hand, he does not talk much about things he does not understand, which is a good trait.

Ib.

633. The first-class professional cricketer is usually a well-made, strong-looking man, ranging from two or three and twenty to thirty five, with agreeable quiet manners.

A. G. Steel
The Badminton Library – Cricket (1904)

634. A cricketer's life is a life of splendid freedom, healthy effort, endless variety, and delightful good fellowship.

W. G. Grace
W.G. – Cricketing Reminiscences and Personal Recollections (1899)

635. Most cricketers dislike the thought of change; perhaps because so many suggestions tend to introduce an artificiality into the game at variance with its character, which has been fundamentally the same since the straight blade replaced the crook.

I. A. R. Peebles
Talking of Cricket (1953)

636. Cricket does not demand of her votaries the hollow face and attenuated frame, and too often the undermined constitution, that a long term of arduous training occasionally results in, especially to a youth of unmatured strength; but a cricketer should live a regular life and abstain at table from all things likely to interfere with digestion and wind.

A. G. Steel
The Badminton Library – Cricket (1904)

637. It always surprises me that some people think a world cricketer should give 100 per cent of his effort and concentration every minute he is playing cricket, and then not relax and enjoy himself after. They seem to have strange ideas about how curfews and conferences and controls should fill his time between play. But if a cricketer does not learn early in his life which things do him good and which are bad for his cricket, and for him, then he does not belong in a world-class team.

Sir Garfield Sobers
Cricket Crusader in *The Cricketer's Bedside Book* (1966)

638. When a cricketer is surfeited, try as he may he cannot flog a tired spirit to give of its physical best.

Diana Rait Kerr and I. A. R. Peebles
Lord's 1946–1970 (1971)

639. Despair is almost natural when chances have been missed.

E. F. Benson and Eustace H. Miles
The Cricket of Abel, Hirst and Shrewsbury (1903)

640. In cricket, as in the graver pursuits of life, the willing workman is ever spurred; he may perform labours of supererogation, and his assiduity meets at best with 'mouth honour': let him, however, but relax his muscles – let him but shorten his career to the speed of his fellows, and he instantly sinks below them in the estimation of his employers. Whether in this case, the feeling arise from envy or not, it is hard to decide; assuredly, however, in very many instances, the mill-horse grinder in the track of duty is acknowledged with greeting, while extra merit 'goes out sighing'.

John Nyren
The Young Cricketer's Tutor (1833)

641. The goddess who presides over Cricket loves to bring down the most skilful players.

Thomas Hughes
Tom Brown's Schooldays (1857)

642. The joy of club cricket is enormous and unabated. There is keenness without exaggerated sense of responsibility and happy appreciation of the fact that the object of the game is to make runs, while the bowler gets his chance on pitches which are not absurdly over-prepared.

Sir Home Gordon
Club Cricket in England in *The Times*, 25 May 1937 and *M.C.C. 1787–1937* (1937)

643. The bane of secretaries is eleventh-hour excuses, or none, for not turning up.

Ib.

644. All cricketers are cricketers, none the less so for not being 'first-class', which is no more than a statistical distinction.

John Arlott
An Eye for Cricket (1979)

645. Cricket has achieved its unique place in the English scene because its champions were admired for themselves. They were men of dignity who stood in the eyes of their countrymen for a code of conduct.

E. W. Swanton
A History of Cricket – Volume Two (1962)

646. The key to the health and prosperity of the game is embedded not in rules and regulations but in the hearts and minds of the cricketers of today.

Ib.

647. It was once thought that the universe moved round our earth merely as its accompanying condition, existing simply and solely for the sake of our earth. And so the batsman has been, and generally still is, regarded as the centre of cricket, for whose enjoyment the rest of the players subsist.

E. F. Benson and Eustace H. Miles
The Cricket of Abel, Hirst and Shrewsbury (1903)

648. In the cricket season I learned there was a safe and far-away place on the field called 'deep' which I always chose. When 'Over' was called I simply went more and more 'deep' until I was sitting on the steps of the pavilion reading the plays of Noel Coward, whom I had got on to after Bulldog Drummond.

> John Mortimer
> *Clinging to the Wreckage* (1982)

649. Cricket is a game; the primary object of games is to give pleasure to the players, and it is quite impossible that the same amount of keen gratification can await the stick who never hits as it realised by the man who, though he may only be at the wickets half the time, yet in that time makes at least ten great hits that will realise forty runs.

> Hon. R. H. Lyttleton
> *The Badminton Library – Cricket* (1904)

650. Above all, he must cultivate the moral qualities that of necessity must have a place in such a great, glorious, and unsurpassable game as cricket.

> Ib.

651. We would not say one word against the personal character of the English professional cricketer, for the great majority of this class are honest, hard-working and sober men. We only say that it is not in the interests of cricket that any branch of the game should be left entirely in their hands.

> Ib.

652. Happily there is never the slightest whisper of suspicion against the straightness of our cricket players, and this is entirely owing to the absence of the betting element in connection with the game.

> A. G. Steel
> *The Badminton Library – Cricket* (1904)

653. Among the crowds of spectators are old cricketers by their hundreds, famous professionals or amateurs whose joy is to watch cricket and reminisce about the great cricket of the past. Some of them are encyclopaedic in their knowledge of figures and performances of the past. Some offer a great deal of information but remember a lot of it not quite correctly.

> Sir Henry Leveson Gower
> *Off and On the Field* (1953)

654. A true cricketer looks to winning the match: the more he contributes to that happy result the more he is gratified, of course; but if presented with a pair of spectacles, his nose will not shrink from its burden if his side wins by even so short a run.

'Quid'
Jerks in from Short Leg (1866)

655. There are no more excellent fellows than the modern cricketer: no better sportsmen and no better company.

E. W. Swanton
Cricket and the Clock (1952)

656. Dullness at cricket comes out of the souls of the players.

Sir Neville Cardus
Good Days (1934)

657. Bowling has its thrills in plenty. It is a great feeling to be able to test a batsman, and find out what sort of ball he does not like, and suddenly to let him have it.

H. M. Herman
How's That? (1937)

658. If a cricketer wants safety and security then let him go into a bank and work. If he's going to play cricket then let him enjoy the game and entertain the public.

Margaret Hughes
All on a Summer's Day (1953)

659. It stands to reason that cricket dominated by amateurs must be livelier than cricket in which professionals (though there are many exceptions among these) set the tone.

Sir J. C. Squire
Introduction to Cardus' *Cricket* (1930)

660. The real fault of the amateurs is that they do it all for nothing; they must be enjoying themselves, and we cannot bear it.

Ib.

661. Condemned to stay at home, he had at once begun to take his bats from their corners and was to be seen in one of the gardener's sheds wiping them and estimating their oiliness.

Charles Morgan
Portrait in a Mirror (1929)

662. I have always helped an opponent to obtain something he will remember all his life if it did not involve any risk to my side losing the match.

Lord Hawke
Recollections and Reminiscences (1924)

663. It does not always follow that a player's behaviour on the field is a true index of his character off it.

Alan Gibson
Jackson's Year (1965)

664. One thing that struck me at once was the fellowship of first-class cricketers. It was a fellowship into which one was immediately included by playing county cricket and by no other means. Until you played you were out: once you had played you were in. You were called by your first name by all in this fellowship from that point on.

T. C. Dodds
Hit Hard and Enjoy It (1976)

665. I see them in foul dug-outs, gnawed by rats,
And in the ruined trenches, lashed by rain,
Dreaming of things they did with balls and bats.

Siegfried Sassoon
The Dreamers (1917)

666. The uplifting, invigorating effect of just one new player in the side! He does not have to be of outstanding ability or personality. He simply needs to be a little different from the others; to possess an aura about him, some quality of remoteness that must cause all those as yet unfamiliar with the man to pause and wonder. Of course the times also have to be propitious.

Edward Docker
History of Indian Cricket (1976)

667. It is not altogether an advantage when a side becomes heavily dependent on one man, however gifted. If he succeeds, he inspires his fellows beyond their normal abilities; but if he fails, he is apt to depress them far below what they can really do.

Alan Gibson
Jackson's Year (1965)

668. Countless are the excuses we hear to cover the feebleness and incapacity of would-be players, made sometimes by their parents, sometimes by themselves.

R. A. H. Mitchell
The Badminton Library – Cricket (1904)

669. The tone suggests some justification for the friends who said that Hyndman, a cricketer, had adopted Socialism out of spite against the world because he was not included in the Cambridge eleven.

Barbara Tuchman
The Proud Tower (1966)

670. 'It's perhaps not necessary,' he said, in gentle reproof, 'to specify every squalid task that falls to the lot of man. That would not be seemly. One's point is that they who do these things are men and women like ourselves. The same sun shines on us all. The same hopes and fears agitate our bosoms. I am no Radical, Anthea: you know that. But I do not hesitate to say that in some sense, despite all diversity of talent and occupation, all men are brothers.'

'*You* can say that, Silvester? And you so different? That's noble of you.'

'Ah, my love,' he said, 'you think too well of me. You can never forget that I made a century in a university match.'

'No, Silvester, I wasn't thinking of cricket. You're too modest.'

Gerald Bullett
Cricket in Heaven (1949)

671. 'Yes, my Anthea, the high gods are just. They play the game. There is – how shall I put it? – cricket in heaven.'

Ib.

672. The wonder is that such a lot of good cricketers evolved from a world so clouded with misconceptions.

C. B. Fry
Life Worth Living (1939)

673. Thus perhaps the best – indeed, the only true – measurement of any cricket performance is made by that notoriously fallible and variable computer, human judgment.

Diana Rait Kerr and I. A. R. Peebles
Lord's 1946–1970 (1971)

674. Figures are not entirely conclusive especially short-term figures, but it is difficult to avoid their significance if a man produces them year after year against every type of opponent and under all conceivable conditions.

Sir Donald Bradman
Farewell to Cricket (1950)

675. The essence of the champion is either inherent in the individual or it isn't, and he prefers to work out a destiny along his own lines.

Jack Fingleton
Cricket Crisis (1946)

676. Few of the great players are deep theorists on cricket, probably because the game has come to them too naturally to need any very close analysis.

E. W. Swanton
Denis Compton: A Cricket Sketch (1948)

677. For cricket is an art in itself. A batsman who is dull and stolid, dour and ungainly, gives little to the game. A great cricketer must be an artist and express himself in his strokes. If he can put all the exhilaration, all the beauty, all the humour and dignity which make up life into his cricket, then he is truly a great player.

Margaret Hughes
All on a Summer's Day (1953)

678. Cricketers of first-class quality need more scope than the one-day match can offer them. Without scope they cannot develop their potential or, having developed, they cannot maintain the standards of which they are capable.

J. M. Kilburn
Overthrows (1975)

679. I have known cricketers who stood head and shoulder above everyone else at net practice, but rarely were able to do themselves justice in a match. Their mental approach to the game was unequal to their natural physical talents.

Sir Leonard Hutton
Just My Story (1956)

680. And finally should you ever reach the dizzy heights of County cricket always reserve your best efforts for Saturdays. You will get your name in the papers twice, on Sunday and Monday.

J. C. Clay
Glamorgan County Cricket Club Year Book (1936)

The Great Players

Denis Compton and Bill Edrich.

Allen, G. O.

681. I like Allen; he keeps the game young, and Test cricket needs reminding now and again that the game began in a meadow and was played by our rude but gusty forefathers.

Sir Neville Cardus
Good Days (1934)

682. Allen had one of the most perfect actions imaginable. He was not a big man, but that beautifully geared run-up and delivery enabled him to bowl in the express class.

E. M. Wellings
A History of County Cricket: Middlesex (1972)

683. Allen was a very fine cricketer, better at playing than at administration.

Ib.

Ames, Leslie

684. He was a grand master of two crafts, and was once, I seem to recall, called an 'idle devil' because he didn't take up bowling!

Ted Dexter
From Bradman to Boycott (1981)

685. There have been more spectacular keepers, but few more reliable.

R. L. Arrowsmith
A History of County Cricket: Kent (1971)

686. A beautiful field anywhere, he must be ranked with the world's great all-rounders.

Ib.

687. Batsman-wicket-keeper or wicket-keeper-batsman, there has never been another like him in the annals of cricket.

G. D. Martineau
The Valiant Stumper (1957)

Armstrong, Warwick

688. In his ascendancy he was respected, if not always beloved, at Headquarters, being a determined and somewhat dictatorial man.

Diana Rait Kerr and I. A. R. Peebles
Lord's 1946–1970 (1971)

689. He was a man who spoke his mind and liked to get his way, regardless of sensitive feelings or niceties. As such he was a strong disciplinarian and somewhat dictatorial opponent.

I. A. R. Peebles
Barclays World of Cricket (1980)

690. He wanted his own way and he got it, seeming to care less than most for the diplomatic niceties. Above his great shoulders watchful eyes glinted out of a square-set uncompromising face, which to casual eyes could look cruel.

Ronald Mason
Warwick Armstrong's Australians (1971)

691. Under the harsh up-country brusquerie was concealed a warm and generous kindliness which came much more fully to the surface in his later years when competitive pressures no longer weighed upon him.

Ib.

Bailey, Trevor

692. Trevor always showed infinite capacity for rising to an occasion and he was never perturbed by spectators who might sometimes not appreciate his worth when he took a long time over his runs.

Sir Leonard Hutton
Just My Story (1956)

693. Bailey awoke from an apparent coma to strike a boundary.

P. G. Wodehouse
Dulwich College Magazine

694. Unfortunately he is likely to be recalled in years to come only as a slow scorer instead of what he in fact was, a fine 'team man' and one of the best all-rounders to play for England – a dedicated cricketer fond of the game and believing that to be played properly it must always be played to win.

Richie Benaud
Barclays World of Cricket (1980)

695. His courage was tremendous, his concentration intense, and the Australians good-humouredly admitted that he had been an infuriating opponent to bowl at.

Rex Alston
Over To Rex Alston (1953)

Barnes, S. F.

696. Art, resolution, stamina, he commanded them all. Well might a man who saw him in his prime have found himself saying, 'Here was a Caesar, when comes such another?'

H. S. Altham
Barclays World of Cricket (1980)

697. On the field Barnes radiated belligerency. Like all the best bowling craftsmen he hated batsmen and believed that every ball delivered should be their last. Bradman triumphed mentally over the opposition because he really did regard his wicket as impregnable. Barnes scythed through batsmen because he believed in the divine right of Barnes.

Bernard Hollowood
Cricket on the Brain (1970)

698. In my humble opinion he is, on all wickets, the finest bowler England has ever possessed.

Sir Pelham Warner
The Book of Cricket (1911)

699. Many astute judges of the game have gone on record as saying that, on all wickets, Barnes was the greatest bowler the game has ever known.

Leslie Duckworth
S. F. Barnes – Master Bowler (1967)

Beauclerk, Lord Frederick
700. When years and infirmities stole upon him, he did not desert the scene of his favourite sport, but enjoyed the game and its social qualities as long as health allowed him, leaving behind him a name among cricketers 'familiar as household words'.

Arthur Haygarth
Lillywhite's Scores and Biographies (1862)

Bedser, Alec
701. All through his career, in days of triumph or frustration, Bedser was manifestly a bowler of quality. He never neglected the basics which proclaim that a straight, good-length bowler is a good bowler.

J. M. Kilburn
Overthrows (1975)

Beldham, 'Silver' Billy
702. Still more wonderful is the story of his family. He had thirty-nine children! twenty-eight by his first wife, all of whom died young; eleven by his second wife.

Bishop Henry Montgomery
The History of Kennington and its Neighbourhood (1889)

703. It mattered not to him who bowled, or how he bowled, fast or slow, high or low, straight or bias; away flew the ball from his bat, like an eagle on the wing. It was a study for Phidias to see Beldham rise to strike; the grandeur of the attitude, the settled composure of the look, the piercing lightning of the eye, the rapid glance of the bat, were electrical. Men's hearts throbbed within them, their cheeks turned pale and red. Michael Angelo should have painted him.

Rev. John Mitford
The Gentleman's Magazine (1833)

Benaud, Richie
704. He was the complete captain, an inspiring leader, thoughtful and adroit in the field and a tough competitor.

Colin Cowdrey
Barclays World of Cricket (1980)

705. Benaud has always had the will to challenge the bowler. In fact, he has both as batsman and captain, waged unceasing war against stodge.

A. G. Moyes
Benaud (1962)

Berry, Les
706. He is one who gives an enabling strength to those prepared to fail around him rather than an arresting figure to those who compile the averages.

R. C. Robertson-Glasgow
More Cricket Prints (1948)

Blythe, Colin
707. The very look on his face, the long, sensitive fingers, the dancing approach, the long last stride, the elastic back sweep of the arm before delivery, with the right hand thrown up in perfect balance against it, and the final flick of the left hand as it came over – all these spoke of a highly sensitive and nervous instrument, beautifully co-ordinated, directed by a subtle mind, and inspired by a natural love for its art.

H. S. Altham
A History of Cricket – Volume One (1926)

Botham, Ian
708. Ian did so much in so short a time that his few inevitable set-backs were doubly disappointing.

Alec Bedser
Cricket Choice (1981)

Boycott, Geoffrey
709. Boycott's idea of bliss might be to bat all night (so long as it was not for Mr Packer), having batted all day.

John Woodcock
Barclays World of Cricket (1980)

Bradman, Donald
710. Arguments about who is the best batsman in history are a pointless charade: Bradman is not only the best, he leaves the rest of the field out of sight whether you measure his achievements by his incredible Test average of 99.94 in 80 innings, by the speed with which he scored his runs, by the strength of the bowling which he so ruthlessly slaughtered, or by his unvarying excellence over a twenty-year span.

H. A. Pawson
Runs and Catches (1980)

711. Perhaps his greatest asset was his wonderful eye. He was able to judge the length of a ball exceptionally early in its flight, which enabled him to play strokes which other players wouldn't even attempt. Like all great players, he kept his head perfectly still as the ball came down the pitch so that he could get an accurate focus on the length of the ball.

He would play a ball just short of a length on the off side to wide mid on with the greatest of ease. Often where most batsmen would have played a defensive shot he, without hesitation, would hit the ball to the boundary.

R. E. S. Wyatt
Three Straight Sticks (1951)

712. Millions, who had not a notion of an off-break or a square-cut, knew him only as the International Bogeyman of cricket.

Margaret Hughes
All on a Summer's Day (1953)

713. Bradman never allowed success to inflate his ego, he was too
modest and sensible for that.

Jack Fingleton
Batting from Memory (1981)

714. Bradman, of course, is a tough proposition.

H. M. Herman
How's That? (1937)

715. He brilliantly and decisively achieved the objective he set himself
when he found his feet in first-class cricket – and that was to be, by
far, the greatest run-getter and the greatest holder of records the
game has known. And, in doing that, he gave to the man-in-the-
street the greatest possible value for his admission money and he
brought to cricket the most pronounced publicity the game had ever
known.

Jack Fingleton
Brightly Fades the Don (1949)

716. Don used to be the third in the trio that was Sydney's pride – 'Our
bridge, our harbour and our Bradman'.

Kenneth Farnes
Tours and Tests (1940)

717. But as I have written in another place, 'In the many pictures that I
have stored in my mind from the "burnt-out Junes" of forty years,
there is none more dramatic or compelling than that of Bradman's
small, serenely-moving figure in its big-peaked green cap coming
out of the pavilion shadows into the sunshine, with the
concentration, ardour and apprehension of surrounding thousands
centred upon him, and the destiny of a Test match in his hands.'

H. S. Altham
The Cricketer Spring Annual (1941)

718. The bat was more of a sabre than a pendulum. But if perfect
balance, co-ordination and certainty of execution be accepted as the
principal ingredients of batsmanship, we who watched the Don in
his early manhood will not hope or expect ever to see its art
displayed in a higher form.

E. W. Swanton
Sort of a Cricket Person (1972)

719. A feature of Bradman's genius was always an ability to place a ball between fielders with unerring precision.

Irving Rosenwater
Sir Donald Bradman (1978)

720. No bigger than a cloud the size of a man's hand when he first appeared, he was destined to plague and dominate our bowlers for nearly a quarter of a century, and to write his name in very big letters in the chronicles of the game.

Sir Pelham Warner
Long Innings (1951)

721. He dominated and he dazzled. He defied belief yet inflicted no outrage on cricketing logic or dignity.

J. M. Kilburn
Thanks to Cricket (1972)

Brown, G.
722. Once at Lord's a man tried to stop one of Brown's balls with his coat, and the ball passed through his coat (pushing it aside) and killed a dog behind it instantaneously.

Bishop Henry Montgomery
The History of Kennington and its Neighbourhood (1889)

Budd, E. H.
723. Lord Frederick Beauclerk said of him that he 'always wanted to win the game off a single ball.'

A. E. Knight
The Complete Cricketer (1906)

Cardus, Neville
724. His gift was a capacity to invest cricket and cricketers with a heroic stature: he interpreted the feelings of the literate cricket enthusiast and, in doing so, changed the entire shape of writing about the game.

John Arlott
An Eye for Cricket (1979)

Chapman, A. P. F.

725. There have been others who played the game harder – not from a personal angle, but who, having got their opponents down, saw to it that they were given no chance of rising again. But I will say this about him, he was one of those majestic personalities who are conspicuous by their absence from present-day cricket.

Leslie Ames
Close of Play (1953)

726. He won or lost with equally good-natured grace.

I. A. R. Peebles
Barclays World of Cricket (1980)

727. In later years he tended to drink more than was good for him and he became a sad shadow of the Adonis who had once been a true national hero. People who had once flocked to be near, now avoided him.

Christopher Martin-Jenkins
The Complete Who's Who of Test Cricketers (1980)

Chappell, Ian
728. A cricketer of effect rather than the graces.

John Arlott
An Eye for Cricket (1979)

Clarke, William
729. But as the years went on the old gentleman dropped down to the last place of all; and being run out by the batsman at the other end (old Tom Box) when it came to the second innings he put on his pads to go in *first*, swearing he would never again go within ten of the fool who had run him out in the previous innings.

Richard Daft
Kings of Cricket (1893)

Compton, Denis
730. Indeed the whole essence of his cricket depends upon his sense of values being qualitative rather than quantitative.

E. W. Swanton
Denis Compton: A Cricket Sketch (1948)

731. One of his captains describes him as the best *teaser* of cover-point he has ever seen.

Ib.

732. Never was such a hero as Denis Compton in those first post-war years: never has Lord's rung to such affectionate applause.
E. W. Swanton
A History of Cricket – Volume Two (1962)

733. Above Hammond even! Yes, and looking back I still think so: not perhaps as an all-round cricketer, but, for all Hammond's superb skill, *as a Test batsman* against the best bowling.
E. W. Swanton
Cricket from all Angles (1968)

734. Denis Compton, although not as sound as Hutton, is a bit of a genius with the bat. He has an extremely attractive presence and he is always completely unaffected by any occasion. In some ways he is almost inconsequential.
R. E. S. Wyatt
Three Straight Sticks (1951)

735. Whereas the methodical runner is like a traveller who consults weather, routes and timetables Denis was more akin to the lover of nature who, seeing a glimpse of sunshine, snatches up his hat and sets out just for the joy of life.
I. A. R. Peebles
Denis Compton (1971)

736. Middlesex have not since produced players with the same magnetism, and Lord's has been the poorer.
Diana Rait Kerr and I. A. R. Peebles (of Compton and Edrich)
Lord's 1946–1970 (1971)

737. My favourite bowler for the desert island of my mind is Grimmett, the two cricketers I would bequeath to schoolboys yet unborn, Compton and Keith Miller. The sun was afraid not to shine when they strolled on to a cricket field.
Kenneth Gregory
In Celebration of Cricket (1978)

738. Many other players have batted excitingly or skilfully or bravely – and Compton's batting has had all three of these qualities – but he is rare in the gaiety which seems to emanate from his play so that all but the most partisan of spectators have felt a liking for him completely divorced from statistics, scores, failure or success.
John Arlott
Cricket (1953)

739. The chief difference lay in the fact that Bradman always applied himself with a cool, unwavering concentration, while Compton seemed to be borne along by a carefree joy. This difference was best illustrated in their running between the wickets. Bradman was fast, decisive and an unfailing judge of speed and distance; Compton was so joyously haphazard that John Warr remarked that his call was merely an opening bid.

Diana Rait Kerr and I. A. R. Peebles
Lord's 1946–1970 (1971)

Constantine, Learie
740. Contrary to all belief, popular and learned, Constantine the magician is the product of tradition and training.

C. L. R. James
Beyond a Boundary (1963)

741. Constantine, the heir-apparent, the happy warrior, the darling of the crowd, prize pupil of the captain of the West Indies, had revolted against the revolting contrast between his first-class status as a cricketer and his third class status as a man.

Ib.

742. No one could appear to play more gaily, more spontaneously, more attractively, than Constantine. In reality he was a cricketer of concentrated passion, irked during all his big cricket life by the absence of what he found only when he played with Shannon. Shannonism symbolised the dynamic forces of the West Indies yesterday.

Ib.

743. He wanted to field all the time, everywhere, and there were many moments when he appeared to be doing just that.

J. M. Kilburn
Overthrows (1975)

744. For Constantine made himself for all predictable time into the great representative symbol of West Indian cricket, partly by the accident of history and partly by the sheer stunning impact of skill and personality.

Ronald Mason
Sing All a Green Willow (1967)

Cowdrey, Colin

745. What is a far greater tribute, in an age when, if one may believe journalists and the endless stream of worthless books published under the names of prominent players, cricket at the top level is a mass of petty jealousies and enmities, is that one never hears Colin mentioned personally without the greatest affection and respect.

R. L. Arrowsmith
A History of County Cricket – Kent (1971)

746. Cowdrey was long one of the world's greatest bats, yet had he given full play to his natural abilities he could have been even greater.

R. L. Arrowsmith
Barclays World of Cricket (1980)

747. Cowdrey, even in youth, was liable to long spells of introspection, of self-doubt.

Alan Gibson
The Cricket Captains of England (1979)

Dexter, Ted

748. He is a temperamental cricketer, and temperamental cricketers depend on the stars being right for them.

Alan Ross
Australia '63 (1964)

749. He was a controversial character and an exciting batsman, the ideal mixture. In full flow it was not too much to claim that he was worth at least double the admission price.

Trevor Bailey
The Greatest of My Time (1968)

Douglas, J. W. H. T.

750. Douglas was a man of character. He possessed courage and determination in a marked degree, and was always the essence of fitness.

Sir Pelham Warner
Long Innings (1951)

751. He had a magnificent physique, it is true, but little natural gift for either sport.

Charles Bray
Essex County Cricket (1950)

752. The harder the job and the tougher the opposition, the more tenacious he became and the more his bulldog spirit showed itself.

Ib.

753. He was a strict disciplinarian. He lived for cricket and he thought all others should have the same enthusiasm, the same keenness and the same guts that he had.

Ib.

754. He was not a great captain, but he was most assuredly a great man and, if he was not an attacking batsman, a persistently attacking bowler.

Dudley Carew
To the Wicket (1946)

755. Tact may not always be his characteristic, and as a captain he is not resourceful or very observant, but as a hero of the cricket-field there have been few who have done more valuable hard work.

Lord Hawke
Recollections and Reminiscences (1924)

Duckworth, George

756. Duckworth's appeals became a feature of cricket at Old Trafford and all other cricket grounds upon which he appeared. It was not so much an appeal as an assertion. He was directing the umpire in his bounden duty and he wanted his decision to be known far beyond the boundaries of Stretford, to say nothing of echoing up and down the Warwick Road line.

John Marshall
Old Trafford (1971)

757. No Lancashire player has been so abundantly Lancashire, no stumper has been more nimble and certainly none more vocal.

Ib.

758. I think I was the first man he ever stumped at Old Trafford; it was a so-called friendly match, and when I missed the ball and Duckworth shrieked his appeal and swept up all the bails and the stumps, I felt as though I had been sandbagged.

Sir Neville Cardus
Second Innings (1950)

Edrich, Bill

759. But Bill was a popular cricketer not so much for his successes as for his repeated triumphs over prejudice and adversity. His pugnacity and aggression, allied to the serene temperament and natural manners which characterise all the Edriches, were there for all to see.

Ralph Barker
The Cricketing Family Edrich (1976)

760. Relishing a scrap, he never gave up in any game until the last entry was made in the scorebook.

John Warr
Barclays World of Cricket (1980)

Emmett, Tom

761. There was no brighter spirit in the field, and there was none more willing. He worked heart and soul in every department of the game, and was always ready to do a spell of bowling to oblige anyone.

W. G. Grace
Cricket (1891)

762. He was popular because of his enthusiasm for play; he was memorable because of his sharp wit, uninhibited comment and unfailing readiness to make good-humoured capital from his own discomfiture.

J. M. Kilburn
A History of Yorkshire Cricket (1970)

Evans, Godfrey

763. He is by far the most energetic keeper I have ever seen. He seems prepared not only to do his own particular job of work but also to relieve the in-fieldsmen of some of theirs.

W. J. O'Reilly
Cricket Conquest (1949)

Fender, Percy

764. He hated the dull finish, the formal declaration, the expected stroke, the workaday over. He rescued treasures of cricket from dust and oblivion, snatched off the covering, and showed them to an astonished and delighted public.

R. C. Robertson-Glasgow
More Cricket Prints (1948)

765. The greatest captain of his time.

J. L. Carr
Carr's Dictionary of extra-ordinary English Cricketers (1977)

Freeman, 'Tich'
766. There was something grotesque in the way the little gnome of a man came rocking up to the stumps, and flicked one ball after another, all so nearly the same, and yet so vitally different, until the victim would either commit some act of indiscretion or, more probably, fall to his own timidity.

E. W. Swanton
A History of Cricket – Volume Two (1962)

Fry, C. B.
767. Fry could properly be called a polymath, but he was above all a classic.

Alan Gibson
The Cricket Captains of England (1979)

768. His marvellous physique made him impervious to fatigue, his self-control never slackened.

H. S. Altham
A History of Cricket – Volume One (1926)

769. England's captain was C. B. Fry, who has been guilty of thinking quite a lot about cricket in his time, and who, in my humble opinion, would have done better as Sole Selector of the England XI for many years than any Selection Committee has achieved.

E. H. D. Sewell
Well Hit! Sir (1947)

770. He is a nice, good-looking young fellow, who can sing a song and can illustrate a note-book with caricatures of his Dons.

Men of the Day no. 584
in Vanity Fair (1894)

771. He was one of the last of his kind – and certainly the finest specimen of it – the amateurs, the smiling gentlemen of games, intensely devoted to the skill and the struggle but always with a certain gaiety, romantic at heart but classical in style.

J. B. Priestley
The English (1973)

Giffen, George

72. He was not a good captain, as he never knew when to take himself off, and always seemed to think that the best possible change of attack was for him to give up bowling at one end and go on at the other.

W. G. Grace
W.G. – Cricketing Reminiscences and Personal Recollections (1899)

Grace, E. M.

73. The fame of E.M.'s doings spread everywhere, and his style of batting was freely criticised. The critics found fault with his cross hitting, and said he was not above hitting a straight, good-length ball; but all agreed that his hitting was something wonderful.

W. G. Grace
Cricket (1891)

74. So tremendous a player must at any time make a stir in the world of cricket, but the stir that E.M. made was all the greater because of the scandalous manner in which he outraged every law of batting that had hitherto been held sacred.

Bernard Darwin
W. G. Grace (1934)

Grace, W. G.

75. I cannot remember when I began to play cricket. Respect for the truth prevents me from saying I played the first year of my existence, but I have little hesitation in declaring that I handled bat and ball before the end of my second.

W. G. Grace
Cricket (1891)

76. Simple zest was what W.G. brought to cricket. Not all subsequent captains of England have done the same. But those who have, win or lose, are the ones we like the best.

Alan Gibson
The Cricket Captains of England (1979)

77. He was far better known by sight than any man in England.

Bernard Darwin
W. G. Grace (1934)

778. Cricket with W.G. was never a game to be played in deathly silence. His voice was often to be heard on the field, in exhortation or comment.

Ib.

779. To W.G., cricket, being a game, was a vehicle for a practical, rough-and-tumble humour.

Ib.

780. He did not think deeply or very subtly about anybody or anything; perhaps not even about cricket, although his knowledge of it was intuitively profound, his judgment of a cricketer unique.

Ib.

781. He never did what he thought a dishonourable thing, but he had a different standard of honour from our own. I believe that in W.G. was found something of a survival of this older tradition.

Ib.

782. Almost as truly as it was said of Napoleon, did W.G. 'cast a doubt upon all past glory, and render all future renown impossible.'

H. S. Altham
A History of Cricket – Volume One (1926)

783. Finally it may be said of W.G. that he did more to popularise cricket than any man who ever lived: his genial personality, his Jovian form, his inexhaustible vitality and stamina and enthusiasm, all combined with his prodigious prowess to make him the focus for an empire's devotion to the game.

Ib.

784. Grace himself had achieved a synthesis of the batting art, which combined defence and violent attack in such judicious proportions that the bowlers despaired: and his apostles carried his teaching to wherever cricket is played, absorbing on their way, improvements introduced by later masters.

Tom Watson
Ibis Cricket, 1870–1949 (1950)

785. W. G. Grace was an autocrat and liked having his own way.

Ib.

786. Grace's praise demands my song,
Grace the swift and Grace the strong,
Fairest flower of cricket's stem,
Gloucester's shield and England's gem:

E. B. V. Christian
Ode to W.G.

787. Dr W. G. Grace
Had hair all over his face.
Lord! how the people cheered
When a ball got lost in his beard!

E. C. Bentley
W.G. in *Baseless Biography* (1939)

788. 'The Champion', 'The Big 'Un', whose portrait in a pre-existence
may be seen engraved upon Assyrian tablets in the British Museum.

J. L. Carr
Carr's Dictionary of extra-ordinary English Cricketers (1977)

789. Had Grace been born in Ancient Greece the *Iliad* would have been a
different book. Had he lived in the Middle Ages he would have
been a Crusader and would now have been lying with his legs
crossed in some ancient abbey, having founded a great family. As
he was born when the world was older, he was the best known of
all Englishmen and the King of that English game least spoilt by
any form of vice.

Bishop of Hereford
The Memorial Biography of Dr W. G. Grace (1919)

790. W.G.'s batting had grandeur and not elegance. It was massive and
ingenious.

A. A. Thomson
The Great Cricketer (1957)

791. His supremacy rested on two foundations: the first was his superb
physical health from which he drew his quickness of eye, strength
of arm and, above all, his unquenchable energy.

Ib.

792. All his life he was facing the next ball.

Ib.

Leslie Ames – there has never been another like him in the annals of cricket.

793. A famous Liberal historian can write the social history of England in the nineteenth century, and two famous Socialists can write what they declared to be the history of the common people of England, and between them never once mention the man who was the best-known Englishman of his time. I can no longer accept the system of values which could not find in these books a place for W. G. Grace.

> C. L. R. James
> *Beyond a Boundary* (1963)

794. Through W. G. Grace, cricket, the most complete expression of popular life in pre-industrial England, was incorporated into the life of the nation.

> Ib.

795. He seems to have been one of those men in whom the characteristics of life as lived by many generations seemed to meet for the last, in a complete and perfectly blended whole.

> Ib.

796. His humours, his combativeness, his unashamed wish to have it his own way on the field of play, his manœuvres to encompass this, his delight when he did, his complaints when he didn't, are the rubs and knots of an oak that was sound through and through.

> Ib.

797. As a cricketer I do not hesitate to say that not only was he the greatest that ever lived, but also the greatest that ever can be, because no future batsmen will ever have to play on the bad wickets on which he made his mark and proved himself so immeasurably superior to all his contemporaries.

> Lord Hawke
> *Recollections and Reminiscences* (1924)

798. He was not a graceful bat and he was not ungraceful; just powerfully efficient.

> C. B. Fry
> *Life Worth Living* (1939)

799. Above all else, W.G. was a very kind man.

> Ib.

800. None of the English cricketers could waltz like W.G.

> Ib.

801. In my opinion, the two great secrets of his success have been his great self-denial and his constant practice.

Richard Daft
Kings of Cricket (1893)

802. He does not hit at it in the sense of slogging; neither does he appear to play either forward or back; but no matter what the length he is on the ball, and hitting it absolutely at the right moment.

Hon. R. H. Lyttleton
Giants of the Game (1899)

803. He turned the old one-stringed instrument into a many-chorded lyre. And, in addition, he made his execution equal his invention.

K. S. Ranjitsinhji
The Jubilee Book of Cricket (1897)

804. His style is impersonal in its greatness. It is distinguished by breadth and ease, and by the absence of any littleness or flourish. No run is ever got by mere *ficelle*.

Anonymous
Modern Men in *The Scots Observer*

Gregory, Jack
805. He employs his face also to add to the dismay his approach is calculated to inspire.

A. C. MacLaren
Cricket, Old and New (1924)

Grimmett, Clarrie
806. He put the third dimension of length into googly bowling and never sacrificed control in attempts to get greater spin.

Ray Robinson
Between Wickets (1946)

807. For those who love the art of bowling it was, as Professor Moriarty said to Sherlock Holmes, 'an intellectual treat', to watch him in action.

I. A. R. Peebles
Barclays World of Cricket (1980)

808. For Clarrie Grimmett leg-break and googly bowling was the main reason for living. Taking a cricket ball away from Clarrie during a match was like taking a bone from a dog.

R. S. Whitington
Time of the Tiger (1970)

Gunn, George

309. He had originally been destined to be a musician, and he brought to cricket the art and imagination, not to say gentle eccentricity, of the musical profession.

Diana Rait Kerr and I. A. R. Peebles
Lord's 1946–1970 (1971)

310. He would never let a game dominate him. Once at Leicester he was batting when the clock came round to one-thirty. The moment it was one-thirty and the over had been completed he started taking off his batting gloves and began to walk towards the pavilion.

'Where are you going?' said the umpire.

'To have my lunch,' was the reply; 'it's one-thirty.'

'We have our lunch here at two o'clock,' said the umpire.

George Gunn prepared to receive the first ball of the next over. As it came down the pitch he walked straight down the wicket, made no attempt to play the ball at all, and was stumped by yards. As he went by the umpire on the way to the pavilion he said, 'I have *my* lunch at one-thirty.'

R. E. S. Wyatt
Three Straight Sticks (1951)

Hammond, Wally

311. From the moment he walked from the pavilion to begin his innings, he looked the master. Such a giant of the game seemed always to dwarf the rest of the team, and the moment he faced up to bowling that had held difficulties for the other batsmen, that bowling appeared to lose its venom.

Sir Leonard Hutton
Just My Story (1956)

312. For Hammond was majesty and power; Hammond was grace and beauty and courage. One glorious cover-drive from him and I would be content.

Margaret Hughes
All on a Summer's Day (1953)

313. His batting was the result of complete purity of style allied to an exceptionally strong and beautifully-proportioned physique. He could have excelled at any game, and his choice was cricket's good fortune.

E. W. Swanton
A History of Cricket – Volume Two (1962)

814. He expressed himself within the framework of the game as he found it and enlarged its scope by the magnificence of manner. His portrayal of cricket was the thing of beauty that is joy for ever and abundance lay about him from seed time to harvest. Grandeur was his cloak and gratitude for it must be his memorial.

J. M. Kilburn
Cricket – The Great Ones (1967)

815. He was one of those natural athletes, whose reflexes worked like lightning. If he had not been a superlative cricketer he could have excelled as a golfer, a swimmer, a boxer and an Association footballer. All these skills came to him with apparently effortless ease.

A. A. Thomson
Cricketers of My Times (1967)

816. Hammond gave to cricket, and cricket gave to Hammond, everything – except the things he wanted most.

Alan Gibson
The Cricket Captains of England (1979)

Hardstaff, Joseph Jnr.
817. Sartorially, as well as in point of cricket-style, Hardstaff is the most elegant cricketer of his day.

Hon. T. C. F. Prittie
Lancashire Hot-Pot (1949)

Harris, David
818. Harris may be considered the first bowler who knew the power of a good-length ball.

W. G. Grace
Cricket (1891)

819. David Harris used sometimes to walk to the ground on crutches, but bowled splendidly, we are told, when he got warm.

Hon. R. H. Lyttleton
The Badminton Library – Cricket (1904)

320. His balls were very little beholden to the ground when pitched; it was but a touch and up again, and woe be to the man who did not get in to block them, for they had such a peculiar curl that they would grind his fingers against the bat; many a time have I seen the blood drawn in this way from a batter who was not up to the trick.

John Nyren
The Young Cricketer's Tutor (1833)

Harris, Lord
321. Perhaps Harris was a bit of a dictator, but he was eminently just and fair.

Sir Pelham Warner
Long Innings (1951)

322. No cricketer is quicker to congratulate a comrade on a fine performance.

W. G. Grace
Cricket (1891)

323. As for *Lord Harris*, the one quality of good captaincy which he did not possess was that of close sympathy with the side under his command.

P. C. Standing
Cricket of Today and Yesterday (1904)

Hawke, Lord
324. Like Lord Harris of Kent, Lord Hawke has been a capital leader of men. He is one of the very best sportsmen in the county; and it is characteristic of the tone of Lord Hawke that he has insisted upon one dressing-room at Bramall Lane for amateurs and professionals.

K. S. Ranjitsinhji
The Jubilee Book of Cricket (1897)

325. He is a splendid captain, inspiring his men by the example he gives them of pluck and resource.

W. G. Grace
W.G. – Cricketing Reminiscences and Personal Recollections (1899)

326. As a cricketer, he was not up to England standards. In strict terms of cricketing merit, he was not worth his place in the great Yorkshire sides which he captained at the beginning of the twentieth century.

Alan Gibson
The Cricket Captains of England (1979)

827. He led the way in making large and necessary improvements in the lot of the professional cricketer.

Ib.

828. His contribution to the game was great, especially in raising the standard of professional conduct and comfort, together with provision after retirement, but he sometimes dwelt too much in the past, and was not sufficiently receptive of new ideas when conditions were changing.

Sir Pelham Warner
Lord's 1787–1945 (1946)

829. He would not tolerate indiscipline or slackness on the field but, off it, he was the pro's friend and adviser. His was the greatest influence of all in the evolutionary process of raising the status of the professional cricketer from a position serf-like in relation to the gentleman. Autocrat he may have been, but a benevolent autocrat nevertheless.

John Marshall
Headingley (1970)

830. The council chambers of cricket suffered their severest loss when the wickets of these two great Englishmen fell.

E. H. D. Sewell (of Harris and Hawke)
Well Hit! Sir (1947)

Hearne, J. W.
831. Taste and discretion were the essence of his play, and its eclectic beauty was never allowed to degenerate into the merely ornate.

Hon. T. C. F. Prittie
Mainly Middlesex (1947)

832. In entering or resigning the office of bowling, in accepting or inwardly rejecting the judgments of umpires, in benefiting from the vigilance or suffering from the indolence of fielders, he exhibited, as near as cricketer may, a conquest over motion and emotion alike.

R. C. Robertson-Glasgow
More Cricket Prints (1948)

Hendren, Patsy

833. He loved his cricket with all his heart and soul. He did everything spontaneously and wholeheartedly and he seemed to call to us to come and play with him and to have as much fun as he was having.

Margaret Hughes
All on a Summer's Day (1953)

834. He had a good example to show in so many directions: in the cool, purposeful way he set about building an innings; in his footwork and the invariable spirit of counter-attack if the bowling was threatening to take the upper hand; in his zest on the field at all times; and perhaps more than all else, in that quality of dry, philosophical humour that saves its owner from the danger of ever taking the extremes of fortune *too* seriously. Cricket was always a game for Patsy, whether he made 0 or a hundred, and it has always been a game with Denis.

E. W. Swanton
Denis Compton: A Cricket Sketch (1948)

835. He liked slapstick, but he knew when and at whom to throw the pie. His short, square build, busy movements, and low-geared run were made for comedy.

R. C. Robertson-Glasgow
Cricket Prints (1943)

836. He had a gift for apt and spontaneous buffoonery, with the instinctive gift for timing and restraint of the accomplished clown who is sensitive to his audience and never persists beyond the moment of discretion.

I. A. R. Peebles
Patsy Hendren (1969)

Hill, Clem

837. He was a man born to lead, but by direct methods rather than by finesse. He attacked frontally, never sought to flank. He would go straight through a difficulty. No situation was too difficult to face or to solve.

A. G. Moyes
A Century of Cricketers (1950)

Hirst, George

838. Hirst is full of the true sporting spirit, the spirit which never cavils at an opponent's good luck, for it knows such things must needs be, and that on the morrow the best stroke shall yield a wicket; the spirit which feels that if all are important in the hands of fate, our very determination and striving shall be part of that fate; a spirit never relaxing, oblivious alike of anger or biting sarcasm.

A. E. Knight
The Complete Cricketer (1906)

839. Stalwart as the oak, generous, and complete master of his craft, he commanded an affection and respect in all who knew him personally or by repute.

Diana Rait Kerr and I. A. R. Peebles
Lord's 1946–1970 (1971)

840. No bowler ever cared less whether it had rained or not.

E. H. D. Sewell
Well Hit! Sir (1947)

841. In George Hirst's cricket we have, almost perfectly displayed, the outlook of the true cavalier: gay and always attacking.

A. A. Thomson
Hirst and Rhodes (1959)

Hobbs, Jack

842. There was a wisdom so informed your bat
To understanding of the bowler's trade
That each resource of strength or skill he used
Seemed but the context of the stroke you played.

John Arlott
To John Berry Hobbs on his 70th Birthday (16 December, 1952)

843. In play, the salient feature of his cricket was that it seemed so unspectacular: he batted perfectly because he was the perfect batsman. His strokes did not seem startling, but inevitable.

John Arlott
Book of Cricketers (1979)

844. To the man in the street cricket was symbolised by Jack Hobbs, his cheerful face lit by a serene smile, just as it had been by the bearded old giant who never met a photographer without a twinkle in his eye. Alike to the expert and the casual observer he was the epitome of batsmanship. Though the game was his profession Hobbs's standard of values was always qualitative rather than quantitative.

H. S. Altham
A History of Cricket – Volume One (1926)

845. A man of natural dignity, with at the same time an engaging twinkle that revealed a charming and constant sense of humour, utterly unspoilt by success and always prepared to help others, especially the young, he soon became and remained throughout his playing days an ideal support for any touring captain, and the embodiment of the highest standards and values in the game.

H. S. Altham
Barclays World of Cricket (1980)

846. Years ago I was sitting with the late A. A. Milne while Hobbs was batting in a Test Match at Trent Bridge. Milne turned to me and said 'The sound of his bat somehow puts me in mind of vintage port.'

Ben Travers
The Infatuee in *The Cricketer's Bedside Book* (1966)

847. Personally, Hobbs is one of the very best, one of the very few whom popularity has not spoilt in the least.

Men of the Day no. 2283
in *Vanity Fair*

848 . . . was the bridge between the Classic and Modern Periods.

J. L. Carr
Carr's Dictionary of extra-ordinary English Cricketers (1977)

849. We shall think of him, trim and tidy, coming out to open the innings; we shall see the twirling of the bat before each ball, the easy, perfectly poised stance at the wicket, those dancing feet move swiftly back or forward, and we shall dream of him 'burning the grass with boundaries', his bat flashing forth every stroke known to cricket.

J. M. Kilburn
In Search of Cricket (1937)

850. This man was England's greatest professional batsman. He scored over sixty thousand runs, he made nearly two hundred centuries, he was a model for the young and a continual amazement to the old; yet preserved throughout an unhurried quietness, a steady and rooted stability, to which his brilliance was an adornment and not a danger.

Ronald Mason
Jack Hobbs (1960)

Hutton, Len

851. Cricket has always been so much a part of my existence that it has occupied my thoughts to the exclusion of other things, particularly after I took over the captaincy of England.

Sir Leonard Hutton
Just My Story (1956)

852. He is a thoughtful, calculating batsman, shrewdly assessing the dangers and requirements of the situation at all times.

I. A. R. Peebles
Talking of Cricket (1953)

853. Temperament, background, and circumstances combined to mould Hutton so that he is remembered as a player of superb and precise defence, watchful and enduring, accumulating runs from every mistake the attack might make, but seldom dominating and disrupting. But those who have had a glimpse of the dazzling series of strokes he could produce when impelled to do so can only wonder what his career might have been had he played for Sussex as an amateur.

Diana Rait Kerr and I. A. R. Peebles
Lord's 1946–1970 (1971)

854. He brought England back to the forefront of world cricket, and showed to his fellow-players a perfection of technique and a dedicated example that were faithfully followed by his young disciples, Peter May and Colin Cowdrey.

E. W. Swanton
Sort of a Cricket Person (1972)

855. Hutton was a cautious captain. This was in his nature, and even had it not been, the circumstances of his appointment would have pressed him in the same direction. His caution had its dismal aspects, particularly in the slowing of the over-rate.

Alan Gibson
The Cricket Captains of England (1979)

856. Hutton was never dull. His bat was part of his nervous system. His play was sculptured. His forward defensive stroke was a complete statement.

Harold Pinter
Hutton and the Past in *Cricket '72* (1972)

857. He left behind him a notable array of figures, an abiding memory of technique approaching the flawless and a profound influence on the course of Test cricket.

J. M. Kilburn
Thanks to Cricket (1972)

858. . . . left first-class cricket with a feeling of relief rather than regret. He had completed an exhausting journey.

J. M. Kilburn
A History of Yorkshire Cricket (1970)

Illingworth, Ray
859. It is doubtful if anyone else had delved so deeply or so effectively into the tactics of the various forms of the contemporary game.

John Arlott
Book of Cricketers (1979)

Jackson, Sir Stanley
860. All that Jackson did on the cricket field he did so easily that it seemed to be the only thing to do.

E. H. D. Sewell
Well Hit! Sir (1947)

861. On the field his mind was locked in combat, off it he was the most genial of companions and opponents. He was, and looked, every inch a cricketer; every inch a captain of England.

Alan Gibson
Jackson's Year (1965)

862. I think it is no exaggeration to say that he was one of the very best
cricketers – perhaps *the* best all-rounder, saving W.G. – ever to
represent England, as well as being a great gentleman.

Ib.

863. What always impressed me was his tenacity of purpose. He never let
a game go, and always had a grip of it even when at a disadvantage.
Lord Hawke
Recollections and Reminiscences (1924)

864. Tactful and diplomatic and a man of the world, Jackson was a
highly successful captain, and he was a wonderful spinner of a coin.
Sir Pelham Warner
Lord's 1787–1945 (1946)

Jardine, Douglas
865. He was a fine cricketer and a character of granite-like texture.
Diana Rait Kerr and I. A. R. Peebles
Lord's 1946–1970 (1971)

866. He would not have been a popular captain with the public even
without body-line, but he would have been, in his own style, a
pretty good one.
Alan Gibson
The Cricket Captains of England (1979)

867. They assumed at once that Jardine's perfectly legitimate protest was
bad sportsmanship. Alexander then bumped several balls down to
Jardine. Jardine was hit and when he rubbed his hip the crowd
cheered in pleasure. Immediately he stopped rubbing his hip and
prepared to receive the next ball. When he came into the dressing-
room at the close of play it was seen that blood was running down
his leg.
R. E. S. Wyatt
Three Straight Sticks (1951)

868. New Zealand in 1931 was hardly strong enough to test his
leadership qualities to the full, but by his very 'presence' on the
field, by the way his team jumped at the word of command, one
sensed that here was a man in control of the situation.
Edward Docker
Bradman and the Body-line Series (1978)

869. *Il faut cultiver notre Jardine.*

Sir Neville Cardus
Good Days (1934)

870. Alike in tactical skill and in personality, he must rank as one of the great captains: if he demanded much of his men, he never failed to give to them and to the game all that he had himself.

H. S. Altham
Barclays World of Cricket (1980)

Jenkins, Roley
871. Jenkins is the factotum of the Worcester XI and happiest when working. He likes cricket.

Hon. T. C. F. Prittie
Lancashire Hot-Pot (1949)

Jessop, Gilbert
872. Gilbert Jessop was the living embodiment of that sensationalism which will always make the most direct and compelling appeal to the man who pays his shilling and wants his money's worth.

H. S. Altham
A History of Cricket – Volume One (1926)

873. His very stance, like a panther's crouch, bespoke aggression. The secret of his hitting lay in his speed, of eye, of foot, and of hand. He combined in a unique degree strength and flexibility of shoulder, arm and wrist.

Ib.

874. If Mr Jessop's batting is no better than his bowling and fielding, he is scarcely likely to become an acquisition to the western shire.

G. L. Jessop
quoting newspaper report *The Croucher's Debut* in *The Cricketer* (1921)

875. When he came in to bat the whole crowd broke out into an 'audible grin', a fever of expectation which made many spectators almost afraid to look in case something went wrong.

Gerald Brodribb
The Croucher (1974)

876. No man in history has combined so consistent a capacity for the devastating hitting of a cricket ball with such brilliance in stopping and throwing in the field as Gilbert Jessop.

H. S. Altham
Barclays World of Cricket (1980)

King, J. Barton
877. He was very fast, came up very quick from the pitch, and, with admirable length, also had consummate ability to do with the ball what he intended, which is what so many brainy bowlers cannot do.

Lord Hawke
Recollections and Reminscences (1924)

Knott, Alan
878. Small, perky, alert as a cat, he is unmistakable from the farthest corner of a ground, whether crouching low beside the stumps, or poised wide-eyed in front of them, handle of the bat thrust forward, as alive to possibilities of misadventure as a boy playing French cricket on a bumpy lawn.

John Thicknesse
Barclays World of Cricket (1980)

Laker, Jim
879. His subtle variations of flight and spin were a continued source of delight to the connoisseur. He learnt to recognise and exploit the foibles of individual batsmen and was able to adapt his techniques to different circumstances.

Trevor Bailey
The Greatest of My Time (1968)

880. If Jim Laker is to be credited with one outstanding attribute, it must be that of intelligence: and not merely intelligence, but *applied* intelligence.

John Arlott
Cricket: The Great Bowlers (1968)

Larwood, Harold

881. Once, in a County match, when Larwood was in the middle of that glorious run-up, the batsman raised his hand and stopped him. Perhaps the dull reason was simply that he wasn't ready. I think, rather, that the batsman, a humble enough performer, was seized with that last love of life which must have urged victims of old to address some trivial and delaying remark to the executioner. A few seconds later the blow fell, and the bails whizzed past the wicket-keeper.

R. C. Robertson-Glasgow
Cricket Prints (1943)

882. Certainly he is one of the world's great bowlers. What a wonderful action, what accuracy and stamina! I can see him now as I write – a demon of destruction to batsmen, with all the concentrated antagonism that a fast bowler should have.

Kenneth Farnes
Tours and Tests (1940)

883. He was, for certainty, the only bowler who quelled Bradman; the only bowler who made Bradman lose his poise and balance, departing from his set path of easeful centuries into flurried and agitated movements.

Jack Fingleton
Brightly Fades the Don (1949)

884. To have seen Larwood in Australia is to have witnessed one of the greatest of all sporting occasions.

Bill Bowes
Cricket: The Great Bowlers (1968)

Leyland, Maurice

885. He was aware of his own distinction in cricket but he made no parade of it and his comment on other players had to be invited before it was expressed.

J. M. Kilburn
Thanks to Cricket (1972)

886. He seems to withdraw himself altogether from the conflict round him and to be engaged in some solitary meditation of his own.

Dudley Carew
To The Wicket (1946)

Lillee, Dennis
887. Few fast bowlers have had finer physique or technique, or such a gloriously flowing action. He added edge to it; with a hostility to his opponents often theatrical and sometimes offensive. He would have been greater still without that.

John Arlott
An Eye for Cricket (1979)

Lindwall, Ray
888. Lindwall's bowling had the beauty of power under smooth control.

J. M. Kilburn
Thanks to Cricket (1972)

889. I suppose if one were granted one last wish in cricket it would be the sight of Ray Lindwall opening the bowling in a Test Match from the Nursery End at Lord's.

John Warr
Barclays World of Cricket (1980)

890. His skill, unaccompanied by histrionics, was something for the connoisseur to savour.

Christopher Martin-Jenkins
The Complete Who's Who of Test Cricketers (1980)

MacLaren, Archie
891. He was clean bowled on the occasion I have in mind for none, but nobody other than a giant of the game could have made a duck so immaculately. He always played cricket as some proud Roman might have played it.

Sir Neville Cardus
A Cricketer's Book (1922) (also in *Days in the Sun*)

892. To see MacLaren at the wicket was like reading prose in Gibbon. The noblest Roman of them all, magnificent in his ambition and reckless in his sovereignty.

Sir Neville Cardus
Cricket (1930)

893. The grandeur of MacLaren's cricket told of the autumnal purple; the decadence of a long royal line was in his arrogant imperialism.

Ib.

894. And MacLaren, surely he stood for the essential majesty in life.
Today I see him as one who transcended the cricketer's fleeting
hour; the magnificence of his play moves me now like some reckless
squandering of the dignity and spirit of man.

Ib.

895. And each hit by MacLaren's bat was Quixote's lance, and the
bowlers were his windmills.

Ib.

896. Mr. MacLaren was one of the most determined players I have ever
met, and his best cricket comes out when confronted with the
greatest difficulties.

A. A. Lilley
Twenty-four Years of Cricket (1912)

897. He played in the Grand Manner. He lifted his bat for his stroke
right round his neck like a golfer at the top of his full swing. He
stood bolt upright and swept into every stroke, even a defensive
back-stroke, with deliberate and dominating completeness. He
never hedged on his stroke; he never pulled his punches. Like all the
great batsmen, he always attacked the bowling.

C. B. Fry
Life Worth Living (1939)

898. It is commonly remarked of really great batsmen that the better the
bowling the better they play, which means, as a rule, that only the
very best batsmen have many scoring strokes against bowling of the
highest class.

C. B. Fry
Great Batsmen: Their Methods at a Glance (1905)

899. There have been very few finer batsmen to watch. Every stroke was
played in the 'grand manner' with a full back-lift, perfect fluency,
and a free follow-through.

H. S. Altham
A History of Cricket – Volume One (1926)

900. Strategy is the art of choosing an eleven, and somehow he never
seemed to get on with his committee, or they with him; and a
captain who cannot obtain the confidence of his committee and
persuade them of the soundness of his plans or dissuade them from
unsound strategy, or who quarrels with them, may forfeit both
fame and victory. MacLaren was a pessimist by nature, and did not
inspire his men to believe in their own prowess; and to make your
men believe in themselves is a very important factor in cricket
leadership.

Sir Pelham Warner
Lord's 1787–1945 (1946)

Mailey, Arthur

901. He spun the ball till it buzzed like a bee, and released it with the
detached joy of the artist. As such he begrudged no batsman and, if
hit for six, felt that he had at least achieved something.

Diana Rait Kerr and I. A. R. Peebles
Lord's 1946–1970 (1971)

902. His study of the physics and mechanics of bowling was profound,
but to the watching layman it seemed that he dismissed his
opponents with a wide smile that was a googly in its own right. He
was by profession (among other professions) a cartoonist and on a
wicket that would give him a fraction of help, he could make a
caricature of any batting side.

A. A. Thomson
Cricket: The Golden Ages (1961)

Mankad, Vinoo

903. Mankad is not a classic opening batsman; far from it. He stoops
over his bat at the crease, like a cat who has seen its deadly foe, the
dog from next door.

Margaret Hughes
All on a Summer's Day (1953)

May, Peter

904. He played stern cricket and charming cricket.

J. M. Kilburn
Thanks to Cricket (1972)

05. He was a good captain, and a great batsman. I suppose the
hesitations arise because he did not turn out quite as expected. Here
he was, an amateur, a classical stylist, three initials and all,
embodying a return to the old tradition – and, tactically, playing
like a canny old pro.

Alan Gibson
The Cricket Captains of England (1979)

06. May, I should say, is a cavalier batsman and a roundhead captain.

A. A. Thomson
Hirst and Rhodes (1959)

07. And it is a fact that a comparatively small innings by the young
Peter May could show more real cricket than many a fifty from
many another batsman.

A. A. Thomson
Cricket: The Golden Ages (1961)

Miller, Keith

08. Keith Miller is the most unpredictable cricketer I have played
against. I am never quite sure what he is going to do next and I
don't think he knows himself until he is about to do it.

Sir Leonard Hutton
Just My Story (1956)

09. Miller enjoyed the companionship of cricket and he enjoyed the
game for the game's sake. Cricket lovers recognised him as a gay
cavalier and they loved him for it.

Phil Tressider
Keith Miller in *The Cricketer's Bedside Book* (1966)

10. Masculine as Tarzan, he plays lustily. Style suffuses his cricket with
glowing power, personality charges it with daring and knocks
bowling and conventions sky-high.

Ray Robinson
From the Boundary (1951)

Murdoch, W. L.

11. He was an ideal captain, a born tactician, a genial chief, a firm
though gentle ruler, and a man of singular pluck and resource.

W. G. Grace
W.G. – Cricketing Reminiscences and Personal Recollections (1899)

C. B. Fry – he was one of the last of his kind.

Mynn, Alfred

12. He was beloved by all sorts and conditions of men, and he in return seemed to think kindly of everyone.

William Caffyn
Seventy-one Not Out (1899)

13. Not merely was he an excellent and powerful bat, but his bowling came upon the mass of the cricket public with startling effect. There was not anything like it either for extraordinary rapidity of pace with the uphand bowling, or accuracy of length and general steadiness. Ere the batsmen who did not know him could oftentimes get their bats down to play his bowling, the stumps were shivered, or the ball was in the hands of, or past, the 'long stop'.

William Denison
Sketches of the Players (1846)

14. Alfred Mynn captured hearts as well as heads. The very sight of his handsome face and magnificent figure was an attraction and his companionable manner gave him wide popularity among both players and patrons.

J. M. Kilburn
Overthrows (1975)

15. How the hop-men watched their hero, massive, muscular, and tall,
As he mingled with the players, like a king among them all;
Till to some old Kent enthusiasts it would almost seem a sin
To doubt their county's triumph when led on by Alfred Mynn.

William Jeffrey Prowse
In Memoriam, Alfred Mynn, 1807–1861

16. With his tall and stately presence, with his nobly moulded form,
His broad hand was ever open, his brave heart was ever warm;
All were proud of him, all loved him. As the changing seasons pass,
As our champion lies a-sleeping underneath the Kentish grass,
Proudly, sadly will we name him – to forget him were a sin.
Lightly lie the turf upon thee, kind and manly Alfred Mynn!

Ib.
(Last verse also in *Bell's Life* 1861)

Noble, Monty

917. He was, of course, an off-spinner, had all the virtues of length and control, but added to them some curious features which made his bowling different.

John Parker
Cricket Styles and Stylists (1979)

Nyren, John

918. John Nyren himself, who borrowed the pen of Charles Cowden Clarke, was a finely built athlete nearly six feet high. The smile which played around his features and in his small deep-set eyes was sweet and 'sincere as an infant's'. Fond of music and of flowers, regular in his attendance at the Mass as became a 'good Catholic', and a very fine cricketer, particularly distinguished for his ability to 'catch out at the point', he was in truth a splendid 'all round' man, one of those rare natures, who, while not perhaps insensible to the shadows of imperfection which lurk around the best of comrades, are yet carried beyond them by intenser feeling to the brighter lights of character.

A. E. Knight
The Complete Cricketer (1906)

Oldfield, Bert

919. A craftsman with a 'positional sense' so highly developed that he could dispense with acrobatics, he made his catches and stumpings in the most honoured tradition, without showmanship.

G. D. Martineau
The Valiant Stumper (1957)

O'Reilly, Bill

920. To hit him for four would usually arouse a belligerent ferocity which made you sorry. It was almost like disturbing a hive of bees. He seemed to attack from all directions.

Sir Donald Bradman
Farewell to Cricket (1950)

921. When bowling he completely dominated the situation. He roared at umpires and scowled at batsmen. There was no sign of veneer or camouflage when he appealed, nor were there any apologies or beg pardons when the umpire indicated that the batsmen's legs were yards out of line with the stumps.

Arthur Mailey
10 for 66 and All That (1958)

Palairet, L. C. H.

2. Everything Palairet did was gracefully done. He batted gracefully, he shot gracefully, he played golf gracefully, and he danced gracefully. He was a charming man, with a very gentle manner, and the memory of 'Coo' Palairet does not fade even with the passing of the years.

Sir Pelham Warner
Lord's 1787–1945 (1946)

Parr, George

3. He was a nervous and choleric man, but popular with his teams. He had bright blue eyes, ginger hair, mutton-chop whiskers with moustache (or without either, according to his mood), and was not much good at administration and not very patient with those who had to do it. I would guess that he was the kind of man who, in any period, would turn out to be a captain of England at something or other.

Alan Gibson
The Cricket Captains of England (1979)

Peate, Edmund

4. In 1882 he was easily the best bowler in England, his record being 214 wickets for 11 apiece, and it is the opinion of those who have watched Yorkshire cricket most closely and longest, that of the great trinity of slow left-handers, Peate, Peel and Rhodes, the first was also the greatest.

H. S. Altham
A History of Cricket – Volume One (1926)

Peebles, Ian

5. He had a beautifully smooth, rhythmical run-up and high delivery, great power of spin, and that perceptible dip at the end of the flight that made it difficult to judge the length. The best batsmen thought they were 'there', and found to their cost that they weren't.

E. W. Swanton
Sort of a Cricket Person (1972)

Peel, Robert

6. No man took punishment as a bowler better, and it never made him shorten his length or send down a wild ball, but when at his deadliest and congratulated afterwards one could detect no gleam of pleasure in his countenance.

Lord Hawke
Recollections and Reminiscences (1924)

Place, Winston

927. Place is one of those who fight fiercely and readily in that fabled last ditch, but with a very British confidence that he will not die there.

Hon. T. C. F. Prittie
Lancashire Hot-Pot (1949)

Ramadhin, Sonny

928. There is almost a kind of magic in the very name 'Ramadhin'. It seems redolent of mystery and guile.

R. E. S. Wyatt
Three Straight Sticks (1951)

Randall, Derek

929. What will become of him? Oh God of cricket, let it be good, for he has given much to your game.

Robin Marlar
Barclays World of Cricket (1980)

Ranjitsinhji, K. S.

930. Something of the languidity of the Orient and a playfulness akin to jugglery tincture his batting, at times somewhat unpleasantly conveying the impression that he merely toys with, rather than attempts to master, the bowling.

A. E. Knight
The Complete Cricketer (1906)

931. Ranjitsinhji played with an Eastern suppleness and magic; he expressed through the game born at Hambledon his own country's dusky genius.

Sir Neville Cardus
Cricket (1930)

932. In the halcyon summers of the century's first lustre it seemed that neither ever failed. At one end was Fry, with Coeur de Lion's broadsword; at the other, Ranji, like Saladin in *The Talisman* with black magic in his silk wrists which could cut a silk handkerchief in two with a flicker of the scimitar.

Denzil Batchelor
C. B. Fry (1951)

933. He is a slim, exceedingly lithe fellow, whose action in the field generally reminds you of a panther.

Princes no. 19
in *Vanity Fair* (1897)

34. No Englishman could have batted like Ranji. 'Ranji,' said Ted Wainwright once, ' 'e never made a Christian stroke in his life.'

> Sir Neville Cardus
> *The Summer Game* (1929)

35. He has a violent temper, which he generally controls with marked ability and the people idolise him.

> *Princes no. 19*
> in *Vanity Fair* (1897)

36. When Ranji passed out of cricket a wonder and a glory departed from the game for ever.

> Sir Neville Cardus
> *The Summer Game* (1929)

37. He combines an Oriental calm with an Oriental swiftness – the stillness of the panther with the suddenness of its spring.

> A. G. Gardiner
> *Pillars of Society* (1913)

38. At his best Ranjitsinhji was a miraculous batsman. He had no technical faults whatever; the substratum of his play was absolutely sound.

> C. B. Fry
> *Life Worth Living* (1939)

39. It is characteristic of all great batsmen that they play their strokes at the last instant; but I have never seen a batsman able to reserve his stroke so late as Ranji nor apply his bat to the ball with such electric quickness.

> Ib.

40. Although I have never been able to play in the least like him, I have certainly made more runs from the time I began to study the way he used his bat.

> C. B. Fry
> *Giants of the Game* (1899)

Rhodes, Wilfred
41. That valiance of character, the tenacity of purpose would conquer any difficulty in the world.

> A. A. Thomson
> *Cricket My Pleasure* (1953)

942. Hostile meaning behind a boyish face – ruddy and frank; a few such easy steps and a lovely swing to the left arm, and the ball is doing odd things at the other end; it is pitched where you do not like it, you have played forward when you do not want to – you have let fly when you know you ought not; the ball has nipped away from you so quickly; it has come straight when you expected break; there is discomfort.

C. B. Fry
On Rhodes in *Strand Magazine.*

943. I judge Wilfred Rhodes to have been the greatest of all slow bowlers.

A. A. Thomson
Cricket: The Golden Ages (1961)

944. If ever there was a *complete* cricketer, it was Wilfred Rhodes: bowler, batsman, fielder and strategist.

A. A. Thomson
Hirst and Rhodes (1959)

Richards, Viv
945. There is a patrician arch to his nose: an unquenchable flash of joy in his smile; an almost languorous air of relaxation in all but the most urgent of his movements. He has not been arrogant in success, which could prove insurance against depression when, as even the greatest have found at times, the roads about the crease are not always paved with fours and sixes.

John Arlott
Book of Cricketers (1979)

Richardson, Tom
946. There was no position a fast bowler could aspire to that he did not attain again and again, and his records are without parallel.

A. A. Lilley
Twenty-four Years of Cricket (1912)

Robins, R. W. V.
947. No cricketer ever brought to the game a more propitious mixture of devotion, enthusiasm, knowledge, and humour.

Diana Rait Kerr and I. A. R. Peebles
Lord's 1946–1970 (1971)

48. He has all the spirited vibrance of jazz, its jerk and starts, its nervous ecstasies and emotional supercharge. He has its erratic measure and its lack of rounded, classical finish. He has, in fact, all of its virtues and some of its faults.

> Hon. T. C. F. Prittie
> *Mainly Middlesex* (1947)

49. However big the crowd or serious the occasion there is something about the cricket of Walter Robins which suggests half-holidays and kicking your hat along the pavement. Perky is the word.

> R. C. Robertson-Glasgow
> *Cricket Prints* (1943)

Robinson, Emmott

50. Emmott was all Yorkshire, dedicated, fanatical. Cricket was his religion and cricket was Yorkshire cricket.

> John Marshall
> *Headingley* (1970)

Sellers, A. B.

51. At times almost a caricature of the Yorkshireman he wanted to be, once he had found his feet he drove his side hostilely: over-aweing, and all but demolishing, many of their opponents.

> John Arlott
> *An Eye for Cricket* (1979)

52. Sellers became a captain of distinction because he played an essential part willingly and to a degree 'beyond the call of duty'.

> J. M. Kilburn
> *Cricket: The Great Captains* (1971)

53. It is all part of the Yorkshire philosophy that if a game is worth playing it is worth playing *hard*, and it was part of the Sellers philosophy that the laws were made to ensure that the battle went to the strong.

> A. A. Thomson
> *Cricket: The Great Captains* (1965)

Shrewsbury, Arthur

54. If ever there was a batsman who never took a risk it was Arthur Shrewsbury. He should have been permanent president of any or all Anti-Gambling Societies.

> E. H. D. Sewell
> *Well Hit! Sir* (1947)

955. A dignity and a grace characterised the man and his cricket.

A. E. Knight
The Complete Cricketer (1906)

956. A great player on all wickets, it was on difficult pitches that he was seen at his very best; his mastery of the back-stroke: his capacity for watching the ball right on to the bat; his inexhaustible patience – these combined to make him possibly as great a batsman on sticky wickets as has ever lived.

H. S. Altham
A History of Cricket – Volume One (1926)

957. Shrewsbury was the most modest and unassuming of men, but he played the game with intense earnestness and seriousness.

Sir Pelham Warner
Cricket Reminiscences (1920)

Small, John
958. Here lives John Small
Makes bat and ball
Pitch a wicket, play at cricket
With any man in England.

Shop Sign quoted in John Nyren's
The Young Cricketer's Tutor (1833)

959. His life was like his innings, long and good,
Full ninety summers he had death withstood.
At length the ninetieth winter came, when (fate
Not leaving him one solitary mate)
The last of Hambledonians, old John Small,
Gave up his bat and ball, his leather, wax and all.

Pierce Egan
John Small, 1737–1826

Smith, Jim
960. Smith brings back memories of provincial music halls, of whelks, and pints of old and mild.

Kenneth Gregory
In Celebration of Cricket (1978)

Spofforth, F. R.

561. His pace was terrifically fast, at times his length excellent, and his breakbacks were exceedingly deceptive. He controlled the ball with masterly skill, and if the wicket helped him ever so little was almost unplayable.

W. G. Grace
W.G. – Cricketing Reminiscences and Personal Recollections (1899)

Steel, A. G.

562. He was, if it is fair to judge by brilliant performances which do not sweep across long years, the greatest amateur bowler England has possessed, the conjunction of the mental and physical giving him fecundity of artifice which Lohmann himself scarcely excelled; and his batting was equally characteristic.

A. E. Knight
The Complete Cricketer (1906)

Stephenson, J. W. A.

563. He is a good, old-fashioned, forward-playing batsman, but dangerous for a partner with short legs or a weak heart.

R. C. Robertson-Glasgow
Cricket Prints (1943)

564. For here is a cricketer to whom the game was the best thing in life; who kicked cynicism and smugness violently aside; who evidently and unashamedly thought cricket 'fit to employ all the heart and the soul and the senses for ever in joy'; who could and would bowl all day with a sort of ferocious accuracy; who danced with delight when he flattened a stump, slapped umpires on the back, ran three when the book said two, and was probably known by his first name to the sparrows in the deep-field.

Ib.

565. In the field his acrobatics only seemed extraordinary when he first came to light, and before it was realised that such efforts were the spontaneous manifestations of one with a unique passion for the game.

E. W. Swanton
A History of Cricket – Volume Two (1962)

566. He did really tear his hair, he did really leap off the ground like some figure in a mad Frederick Ashton cricketing *ballet*.

Dudley Carew
To the Wicket (1946)

Surridge, W. S.

967. His drive and his bubbling enthusiasm made Surrey into a
ruthlessly efficient side and undoubtedly put him among the
outstanding county captains of history. Not the least of his
achievements was the way in which he made the most of his own
limited talent with bat and ball.

E. W. Swanton
A History of Cricket – Volume Two (1962)

Sutcliffe, Herbert

968. Herbert Sutcliffe made himself an integral part of Yorkshire cricket.
He served its cause and honoured its traditions, but he was not a
passive accepter. He elevated the cause and enlarged the traditions.

J. M. Kilburn
Thanks to Cricket (1972)

969. He lived a corporate life in splendid isolation.

Ib.

970. His great strength lay not only in the quickness of eye and bodily
reaction that accompany all conspicuous batting skills, but in his
famous imperturbability of temperament.

Ronald Mason
Sing All a Green Willow (1967)

971. Proficiency demands concentration of the highest order, and
Herbert had more of this than anyone else I know.

Sir Leonard Hutton
Just My Story (1956)

Tate, Maurice

972. It was as if bowling had been implanted in him at birth, and came
out – as the great arts come out – after due digestion, at the peak of
greatness which is not created – but only confirmed – by instruction.

John Arlott
Cricket Heroes (1959)

973. Maurice Tate did not merely play cricket; he lived in it.

Ib.

974. For Maurice Tate it was who personified Sussex cricket, and
throughout a long precious exciting day he seemed always to be at
the centre of things.

Gerald Brodribb
Maurice Tate (1976)

Taylor, Tom
975. Taylor was a brilliant but uncertain batsman, a superb and tricky
fieldsman, but one in whose heart was no guile.

A. E. Knight
The Complete Cricketer (1906)

Trott, G. H. S.
976. In the opinion of many players associated with him, Australia never
had a better captain and, with his understanding of the personalities
and problems of members of his team he had a unique advantage
over some later leaders of Australia's Test elevens.

Robert Trumble
The Golden Age of Cricket (1968)

Trueman, Fred
977. Apart from his natural aptitude, he became a great fast bowler for
two reasons. The first was his single-minded determination to be
exactly that; the second, his immensely strong body. It was not
merely powerful, it was quite phenomenally solid, without
observable weakness; and it proved magnificently durable.

John Arlott
Fred (1971)

978. Trueman's cricket drew response from both student and the simpler
spectator. His bowling gave satisfaction through its vigour and by
its sophistication. Greatness was in him and it was not obscured.

J. M. Kilburn
A History of Yorkshire Cricket (1970)

Trumper, Victor
979. But never have I felt the pride of life to open and to flow more
grandly and sweetly and graciously than I feel it today as I call back
to mind the batsmanship of Victor Trumper.

Sir Neville Cardus
Good Days (1934)

980. His whole bent is aggressiveness towards the bowling, and he plays
a defensive stroke only as a very last resort.

C. B. Fry and G. W. Beldam
Great Batsmen – Their Methods at a Glance (1905)

981. Many great players have illustrated the game of cricket: of
Trumper, more than anyone, it may be said that he adorned it.

Alan Gibson
Jackson's Year (1965)

982. But then no rules, no generalisations can ever be applied to Trumper. He will always be the most enchanting, and the most maddening, cricketer of them all.

Ib.

983. His timing has never been excelled, and in the art of placing the ball he was unsurpassed.

F. S. Ashley-Cooper
Cricket Highways and Byways (1927)

984. From start to finish of the season, on every sort of wicket, against every sort of bowling, Trumper entranced the eye, inspired his side, demoralised his enemies, and made run-getting appear the easiest thing in the world.

H. S. Altham
A History of Cricket – Volume One (1926)

985. In Victor Trumper we have seen the very poetry and heard the deep and wonderful music of batsmanship.

A. E. Knight
The Complete Cricketer (1906)

986. With luxuriant masterfulness, yet with the unlaboured easy naturalness of a falling tear, or rather of showers from the sunny lips of summer, he diverted the ball in every conceivable direction which his genius willed.

Ib.

987. It reminds one of Victor Trumper's magic wand waving o'er the Sydney crowd, lifting their affections into the greatness of a common joy.

Ib.

988. Victor Trumper had the greatest charm and two strokes for every ball.

C. B. Fry
Life Worth Living (1939)

989. As he walked past me he smiled, patted the back of his bat and said, 'It was too good for me.' There was no triumph in me as I watched the receding figure. I felt like a boy who had killed a dove.

Arthur Mailey
10 for 66 and All That (1958)

Tunnicliffe, John

990. For years he was a solid rock upon which many a new ball wasted itself in vain, and it is doubtful whether any better professional batsman has ever been denied representative honours.

H. S. Altham
A History of Cricket – Volume One (1926)

Tyldesley, Richard

991. Rich humour and ripe skill made up his cricket, and he left behind him much to remember and love.

R. C. Robertson–Glasgow
More Cricket Prints (1948)

Verity, Hedley

992. Verity counted cricket both a privilege and an obligation and bowling a proper subject for serious study.

J. M. Kilburn
A History of Yorkshire Cricket (1970)

Wadekar, Ajit

993. At least he could console himself that his record had never been even remotely approached by any other captain of India, nor was likely to be in the forseeable future. A capable and conscientious skipper who had played the game according to his lights, his departure would leave a serious hole in the batting at least.

Edward Docker
History of Indian Cricket (1976)

Walters, C. F.

994. He walked to the wicket like a free man, one going out to a hard, but agreeable task.

R. C. Robertson–Glasgow
More Cricket Prints (1948)

Ward, William

995. I have not seen much of your playing – certainly not so much as I could have wished; but, so far as my observation and judgement extend, I may confidently pronounce you to be one of the *safest* players I remember to have seen.

John Nyren
The Young Cricketer's Tutor (1833)

Warner, Sir Pelham

996. Among the figures that challenge oblivion in the long vistas of the game – W.G., with his black beard and M.C.C. cap, Ranji, in his fluttering sleeves of silk – few surely were more familiar, none certainly was better loved, than that of 'Plum' Warner, the 'Happy Warrior', in his Harlequin cap.

H. S. Altham
A History of Cricket – Volume One (1926)

997. He was a great captain. His methods were gently persuasive rather than fire-eating, but no tactician ever exceeded his shrewdness and his alert grip of the momentary situation, nor his knowledge of the foibles of friend and foe alike.

Diana Rait Kerr and I. A. R. Peebles
Lord's 1946–1970 (1971)

998. Warner was the quiet gentle-mannered type of skipper, who had no need to drive his men to get the best out of them. He was one under whom they liked playing, and inevitably they played their hardest for him. His own cricket set an example of grit and determination, and he was an optimist who could visualise eventual victory in the most forbidding circumstances.

E. M. Wellings
A History of County Cricket – Middlesex (1972)

Washbrook, Cyril

999. His square-cut was like the quick fell of a headsman's axe, clean and true.

Margaret Hughes
All on a Summer's Day (1953)

1000. His is an uncomplaining, unswerving character.

Hon. T. C. F. Prittie
Lancashire Hot-Pot (1949)

Woods, S. M. J.

1001. Everyone loved Sam, for the whole world's manliness and generosity seemed to have gathered into his heart.

R. C. Robertson-Glasgow
46 Not Out (1948)

2. No captain knows more of the game or uses his knowledge better. He has boundless enthusiasm, and the power of infusing a strong solution of it into others. What is more, he tries every ounce, and makes others try also. He thoroughly deserves his enormous popularity.

K. S. Ranjitsinhji
The Jubilee Book of Cricket (1897)

olley, Frank

3. Nobody was ever bored by what Frank Woolley did or said on a cricket field!

C. S. Marriott
The Complete Leg-break Bowler (1968)

4. A glorious upstanding batsman of free-flowing beauty of execution.

Ronald Mason
Plum Warner's Last Season – 1920 (1970)

5. No batsman, whether right-handed or left, has ever made so many runs so consistently over so many years at such a speed and with such ease and grace.

R. L. Arrowsmith
A History of County Cricket – Kent (1971)

6. Even more must it be emphasised that there never was a player whose value to his side is revealed less by the number of runs he made.

Ib.

7. He never played forward for defence, holding that a ball which could be played forward at all could be played with a full swing of the bat.

Ib.

There was all summer in a stroke by Woolley, and he batted as it is sometimes shown in dreams.

1008. It may be said that Woolley was the most graceful of the efficient, and the most efficient of the graceful.

I. A. R. Peebles
Woolley – the Pride of Kent (1969)

1009. He never showed off; it was an attitude of which he was incapable even as a youngster, but it pleased him always to give pleasure, and he left the game before that power in him had diminished. For that reason, he will always be remembered in Kent as a man who retained his youth until his fifties.

Ib.

10. . . . there was all summer in a stroke by Woolley, and he batted as it is sometimes shown in dreams.

R. C. Robertson–Glasgow
Cricket Prints (1943)

1. I hold it better to have seen Frank's swing
And let its fragile beauty magnify
My own poor discord, joyous graceful thing,
Than to have reaped all Painting's harmony.

M. J. C. Allom and M. J. Turnbull
Frank Woolley

2. When he walked in for the last time something went out of cricket which could never be recaptured.

E. W. Swanton
A History of Cricket – Volume Two (1962)

rrell, Frank

3. As Shakespeare said – some men in their lives play many parts. Worrell was one of the few to do it all at the same time.

Clayton Goodwin
Caribbean Cricketers (1980)

4. But it was his leadership, in matter and manner, which marked him as the most remarkable captain of his age.

C. L. R. James
Barclays World of Cricket (1980)

ight, Doug

5. Yet he played repeatedly for England and one suspects that there was relief among the opposition when he was left out. For years there was no bowler in the world against whom the best batsmen felt less secure, none who was more likely to produce a ball which left them helpless.

R. L. Arrowsmith
A History of County Cricket – Kent (1971)

att, R. E. S.

6. But Wyatt's chief limitation is a lack of distinction, an entire absence of elegance and charm. He is a utilitarian batsman.

Hon. T. C. F. Prittie
Mainly Middlesex (1947)

1017. In fact, in four years of parents' matches no one got *him* (Wyatt) out. That, perhaps, is the mental difference between a Test player and a good county player like myself.

H. A. Pawson
Runs and Catches (1980)

Yardley, Norman
1018. I know that all the Australians that have played against him hold him in the highest regard.

W. J. O'Reilly
Cricket Conquest (1949)

Index of Authors

Index of Key Words

Classic
he was above all a c. 767
not a c. opening batsman 903
the bridge between c. and
modern periods 848

Classical
romantic at heart but c. in
style 771

Clay
c. in the soil has always
handicapped the ground
men 336

Climate
Australian c. 263

Cloud
no bigger than a c. the size
of a man's hand 720

Club
I love the old c. 324
might well have been forced
to it by watching c.
cricket 474

Clubs
swinging Indian c. 5

Coaching
All c. has a tendency at first
to eradicate individual
peculiarities 7
c. is very often necessary 10
c. must somehow be
improved 14
c. which is good 8
there are amenities in c. 9

Cold
such was the c. 401

Coma
awoke from an apparent c. 693

Combines
C. an Oriental calm with an
Oriental swiftness 937

Comedy
Great is the power of c. 859

Commercial
As a c. speculation 287

Community
It is a c., an establishment 341

Complete
a c. cricketer 944

Comradeship
this c. of feeling 463

Concern
an agony of c. 580

Confidence
Very British c. 927

Congratulate
No cricketer is quicker to c.
a comrade 822

Connoisseur
something for the c. to
savour 890

Conquest
a c. over motion and
emotion alike 832

Context
the c. of the stroke you
played 842

Contrast
the present and the past
come in such vivid c. 362

Contribution
His c. to the game was great 828

Control
a man in c. of the situation 868

Dangerous
d. for a partner with short
   legs   963
Such words as 'd.'   310

Debrett
straight out of D.   357

Deep
a safe and far-away place on
   the field called d.   648

Defence
a player of superb and
   precise d.   853
combined d. and violent
   attack   784

Defend
D. until the excitement   66

Defensive
The d. was completely
   unknown   441

Delos
The D. of cricket   368

Democracy
as good a form of d. as
   exists   454

Democratic
a liking for d. ideals   258

Dependent
heavily d. on one man   667

Descent
My sudden d. from cricket's
   pinnacle   455

Desert
he did not d. the scene of his
   favourite sport   700

Design
d. there always is   599

Despair
D. is almost natural   639

Destiny
a moment of d.   600

Deteriorate
Cricket has appeared to d.   519

Determination
single-minded d.   977

Determined
one of the most d. players   896

Detractors
Every age of cricket has its
   contemporary d.   420

Devotion
d., enthusiasm, knowledge
   and humour   947
His d. to the game of cricket   241

Dictatorial
a determined and somewhat
   d. man   688
a strong disciplinarian and
   somewhat d. opponent   689

Differentiating
aims at d. between the
   classes of cricket   482

Dignity
A d. and a grace
   characterised the man   955
A man of natural d.   845
They were men of d.   645

Dilettante
there is a d. look   337

Dimension
He put the third d. of length
   into googly bowling   806

Enchanting
the most e.   982

Endure
Lord's will e.   364

Energetic
the most e. keeper   763

Enjoy
e. cricket in India   290
let him e. the game and
    entertain the public   658

Enjoying
they must be e. themselves   660

Entertainment
provided rare e.   262

Enthusiasm
He has boundless e.   1002
his e. for play   762

Entrance
E. be nothing   325

Entranced
Trumper e. the eye   984

Epitome
the e. of batsmanship   844

Equal
all men in the island are e.   301

Equality
greet one another practically
    on an e.   484

Essential
e. a part of the English
    landscape   297

Example
a great e. to the world   572
He had a good e. to show in
    so many directions   834

Excellence
his unvarying e. over a
    twenty-year span   710

Excellent
an e. and powerful bat   913

Excitement
cricket never was and never
    can be a game of
    continuous e.   598

Excuses
Countless are the e. we hear   668

Exercise
cricket is certainly a very
    good and wholesome e.   570
To take violent e.   256

Existence
so much a part of my e.   851

Expectation
a fever of e.   875

Experiment
ascertained by e.   92

Eye
A cricketer is just a man
    with a clear e.   632
his greatest asset was his
    wonderful e.   711

Fair
as f. and as generous as any
    assembly   528
the chivalrous spirit of f.-
    mindedness   546

Flavour
cricket's f. is so readily
concentrated   350

Flight
whirring f. of a driven
partridge   55

Flush'd
f. with his rays   617

Food
no f. till you're through   597

Fool
never again go within ten of
the f.   729

Forward
Any fool can play f.   30
He never played f. for
defence   1007
It is impossible for f. play   29

Free
He walked to the wicket like
a f. man   994
the first-class game was f.
and fast flowing   444

Freedom
a life of splendid f.   634

French
the F. have never understood
the game   254

Friendliness
atmosphere of tolerant f.   330

Gaiety
rare in the g. which seems to
emanate from his play   738

Gamblers
Australians are notorious g.   271

Game
a clean g. dirtily clad   398
a much-loved g. on grounds
one has known   443
an unfortunate g. for his
Lordship   415
a whole and wholesome g.
of cricket   550
cricket is the greatest
outdoor g. in the world   587
glorious, manly, British g.   615
he has given much to your
g.   929
It's the g. that calls me   506
it was a great g., and
exciting and dramatic   620
not reasonable opportunities
to join in the great
outdoor g.   539
O wonderful g.   592
the g. was the best thing in
life   964
when's the g. itself going to
begin   582

Games
It is the best of all g.   343
should be good g.   551
the g. of the lower orders   498

Gave
G. up his bat and ball   959

Gem
Gloucester's shield and
England's g.   786

Genial
he was the most g. of
companions and
opponents   861

Genius
a bit of a g. with the bat   734
G., however, is a personal
force   434

Grotesque
There was something g. 766

Ground
a pretty well-appointed
   cricket g. 243
most beautiful cricket g. 244

Guile
in whose heart there was no
   g. 975

Habit
this h. comes from keenness
   or mistrust 464

Hand
watching the bowler's h. 28

Happiness
the 'open sesame' to a
   lifetime of h. 347

Hard
it is worth playing h. 953

Harvest
It was like the end of h. 453

Health
The key to h. and prosperity 646

Heart
My h. is as sound as ever 451
so is the strong h. of the
   cricketer 594

Hearts
captured h. as well as heads 914

Heaven
cricket in h. 671
Lord's must be a bit like H. 340

Hero
Never was such a h. 732

Heroes
hailed as h. 260
Those h. dead and gone 432

Heroic
a capacity to invest cricket
   and cricketers with a h.
   stature 724

History
I am stepping into h. 349

Hit
h. the ball hard and enjoy it 622
the big h. 56

Hitter
a most severe h. 62
hard h. 63

Hitting
his h. was something
   wonderful 773
h. it absolutely at the right
   moment 802
the devastating h. of a
   cricket ball 876
The great thing in h. 58
the secret of his h. lay in his
   speed 873

Honest
Cricket in action is as h. to–
   day 486

Honesty
h. of physical endeavour 581

Honour
He had a different standard
   of h. 781

Hope
a h. to the bowler 69

Hoped
Who ever h. like a cricketer 628

Interests
not in the i. of cricket 651

International
i. cricket matches 259

Intolerance
i. of an enemy's prowess 328

Introspection
long spells of i. 747

Irksome
Cricketers, being human,
are not over-ready to do
what is i. 631

Irrational
I had devoted far too much
of my life to this utterly i.
game 517

Isolation
He lived a corporate life in
splendid i. 969

Journey
He had completed an
exhausting j. 858

Joy
borne along by a carefree j. 739
j. is to watch cricket 653
the best j. in cricket 490
the detached j. of the artist 901
the greatest of a common j. 987
the j. of club cricket is
enormous and unabated 642

Joys
the j. of this game are chiefly
these 470

Judgment
beaten essentially by our
defective j. 77
his j. of a cricketer unique 780

Judge
a poor j. of a run 417

Just
eminently j, and fair 821

Justified
a captain is, then, not only
perfectly j. 211

Killed
k. a dog behind it
instantaneously 722

Kind
W.G. was a very k. man 799

Kindliness
a warm and generous k. 691

Kindly
seemed to think k. of
everyone 912

King
like a k. among them all 915

Knocked
it don't like getting k. about 390
knuckles handsomely k.
about 408

Know
What do they k. of cricket 299

Known
far better k. by sight 777

Ladies
l. would be admitted into
the pavilion 479

Livelihood
cricket affords to a race of professionals a merry and abundant though rather laborious l. ... 553

Living
the main reason for l. ... 808

Local
Saturday afternoon l. cricket games ... 249

Love
that last l. of life ... 881
you do well to l. it ... 509

Loved
He l. his cricket with all his heart and soul ... 833
none certainly was better l. ... 996

Lovely
Cricket, l. cricket ... 369
produced one l. thing ... 332

£. s.d.
professional cricket is lapsing into £. s.d. ... 610

Luck
l. plays a bit part in cricket ... 37
l. plays an important part ... 36

Lunch
I have my l. at one-thirty ... 810

Lustily
he plays l. ... 910

Lyre
He turned the old one-stringed instrument into a many-chorded l. ... 803

Magic
a kind of m. ... 928
black m. in his silk wrists ... 932
the name is m. ... 358
There's m. in the names I used to know ... 431
touches their souls with a m. of its own ... 356
weird m. hidden in a leathern ball ... 381

Magnificent
m. in his ambition and reckless in his sovereignty ... 892

Majestic
he was one of those m. personalities ... 725

Majesty
m. and power ... 812
the essential m. of life ... 894

Management
bad m. in the field ... 170

Manliness
m. and generosity seemed to have gathered into his heart ... 1001

Manly
to introduce a m. game ... 293

Man-monkey
when first a m. ... 590

Manœuvre
Every m. must be tried ... 208

Massive
m. and ingenious ... 790

Master
He was a grand m. of two crafts ... 684

Music
nor sweeter m. in the world
   is found 468
the deep and wonderful m.
   of batsmanship 985

Nature
the lover of n. 735

Nervous
a n. and choleric man 923

Net
head and shoulders above
   everyone else at n. practice 679

New
just one n. player in the side 666

Next
All his life he was facing the
   n. ball 792

Nothing
n. ever happens at cricket 480

Oak
an o. that was sound
   through and through 796
stalwart as the o. 839

Objects
main o. of the county club 323

Odds
a man cannot learn the o. of
   cricket 627

Older
o. than the County
   Championship 430

Opponent
I have always helped an o. 662

Outraged
he o. every law of batting 774

Ovation
a standing o. at Lord's 365
received an o. 210

Own
he wanted his o. way and he
   got it 690

Pain
There can be raw p. and
   bleeding 532

Panegyric
a standing p. on the English
   character 554

Panther
reminds you of a p. 933

Passion
a cricketer of concentrated
   p. 742

Past
every feature of a glorious p. 353

Patience
in the matter of p. 292

Pavilions
The rude p. sadden all thy
   greens 250

Peace
a place of infinite p. 351

Perfect
he was the p. batsman 843

Perfection
a p. of technique and a
   dedicated example 854

Save
s. the fours 173

Saved
a run had been s. 180

Science
cricket combines a great
amount of s. with the
advantage of bodily
exercise 593

Scoring
happiest s. mood 48
s. greatly diminished 26

Scrap
Relishing a s. 760

Seam
the average s. bowler 134

Secure
no bowler in the world
against whom the best
batsmen felt less s. 1015

See
can never s. a ball 370

Selection
s. committees are useful
institutions 222

Selector's
a s. job is interesting 219

Self-confidence
s. at cricket 609

Self-control
his s. never slackened 768

Sensationalism
the living embodiment of
that s. 872

Sensitive
the country umpire is a s.
animal 229

Set-backs
his few inevitable s. were
doubly disappointing 708

Shadow
a sad s. of the Adonis 727

Shrewdness
no tactician ever exceeded
his s. 997

Side
the s. was what mattered to
everyone 487

Sight
a pleasant s. it is 335

Silence
never a game to be played in
deathly s. 778

Sixes
the curving flight of s. 425

Skates
the wearing of s. 469

Skill
exacting game of s. 505
the greatest cricket s. 544
you will have to develop an
individual s. 548

Skills
All these s. came to him
with apparently effortless
ease 815
basic s. 438

Slapstick
He liked s. 835

Slipped
Sorry, doctor, she s. 407

Strategy
s. is the art of choosing an
   eleven   900

Strength
one who gives an enabling s. 706
playing s. 35

Stroke
every s. known to cricket 849
never made a Christian s. 934

Study
a proper subject for serious s. 992
his s. of the physics and
   mechanics of bowling was
   profound 902
I began to s. the way he used
   his bat 940

Stumping
s. requires 194

Stumps
the attack and defence of
   three s. 253
the dentist drew the s. 414

Success
they do not achieve their s.
   without toil 22

Succeed
an extra urge to s. there 360

Suffered
s. from captains 216

Suffocation
The modern game was
   gripped to the point of s. 520

Summer
all s. in a stroke by Woolley 1010
Imperial S. bows her golden
   head 424

Sun
The s. was afraid not to
   shine 737

Sunshine
cricket should be played in
   anything but golden s. 605

Suppleness
an Eastern s. and magic 931

Supremacy
His s. rested on two
   foundations 791

Surfeited
When a cricketer is s. 638

Suspicion
never the slightest whisper
   of s. 652

Sweetheart
My only s. is a bag 399

Swerver
Even the best s. 133

Symbol
the great representative s. of
   West Indian cricket 744

Sympathy
close s. with the side under
   his command 823

System
His bat was part of his
   nervous s. 856

Tact
T. may not always be his
   characteristic 755

Tactful
T. and diplomatic and a man
   of the world 864

Tactics
the t. of the various forms of
   the contemporary game 859